LETTERS &
NUMBERS

HOW ENGLISH'S NUMERICAL CODE REVEALS THE SCRIPTING OF HISTORY, NEWS, ELECTIONS, RIGGED SPORTS & MORE . . .

SEE THROUGH FAKE NEWS LIES IN NUMERICAL DISGUISE

"I've never read so little and learned so much. From Roswell & Area 51, to JFK, to the moon landing, to 9/11, to Sandy Hook, and beyond, history's mysteries are connected and solved, definitively."

"Now I know what the film *They Live* and its magic shades were about, it was Kabbalah, Gematria & Isopsephy, the numbers behind the letters! This is a must-read, you'd cheat yourself not to!"

"If your husband reads this, he will get off the couch and give up the sports game FOREVER."

"Revolutionary! The New World Order is finished!"

written by Zachary K. Hubbard, creator of Free to Find Truth

TABLE OF CONTENTS

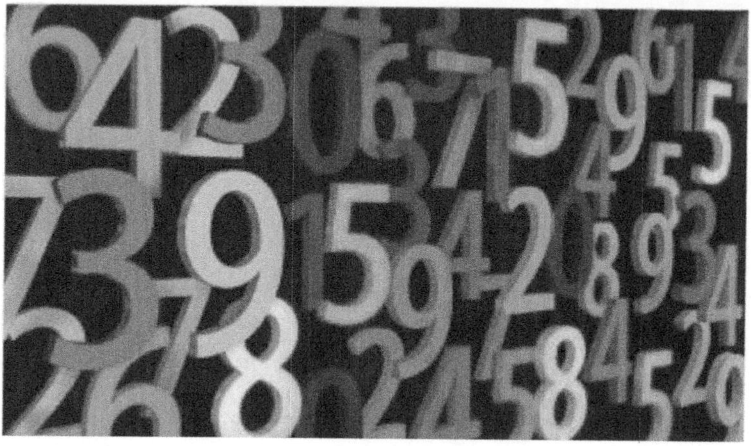

INVITATION TO READER

Those who read and finish this book will gain a new skill and set of knowledge that will empower them for the rest of their life, in more ways than can now be appreciated. Without the knowledge contained in the pages ahead there are doors of understanding about the past, present and future that can otherwise not be attained. This knowledge is owed to every person living, adult and child. It is as simple to learn as elementary arithmetic and as deep as time. My intent as your teacher of this age-old secret is to be as clear, logical, honest, evidence based and intriguing as possible. My hope is you will share this knowledge with your family and friends after you finish reading. The structure is as follows:

Introduction to Letters and Numbers

1. Dedication – For the Truth Seekers

2. Why Are There 26 Letters In the English Alphabet? (The God Code, Letters, Numbers & Bones)

3. The 4 Foundational English Ciphers, Where Geometry Meets Gematria Meets English

4. **What Revelation 13:18 (666, Number of the Beast) Reveals About Mankind, History & the Holocaust**

5. **The Complimentary Ciphers, Tributes to Hebrew Gematria & Greek Isopsephy**

The Personal / Universal Side of the Letters and Numbers Code

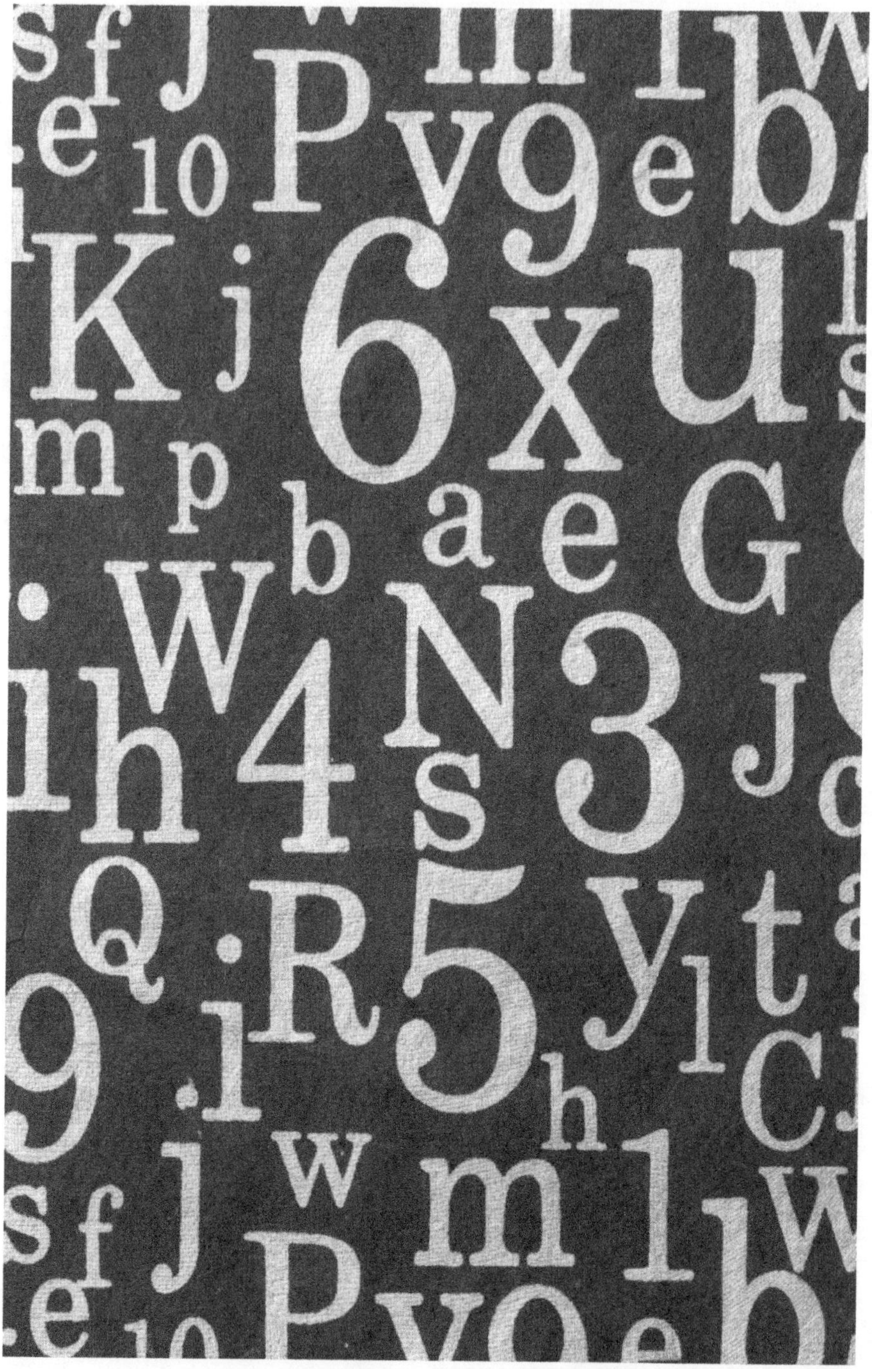

Dedication

For the Truth Seekers, Children & Coincidence Theorists

This book is written for every English speaking person in the world, and I hope to God it reaches the hands of every last person who knows the language. This book is especially written for every truth seeker, who sees the lies being pushed by mainstream media, and *Big Brother,* and is looking for the solution to stop the agenda of deceit that is resulting in the loss of liberties, and our feeling of safety in our own communities. Even more, this book is written for every English-speaking child, who will be brought up in an education system that does not teach the single most important thing there is to know about the language itself, the numerical sequence behind it. Every child, as well as every person who reads this book, will gain knowledge that will advance their understanding of this world in more ways that can now be appreciated. For the child who does not enjoy mathematics, or reading or writing, I imagine they will suddenly find a new heightened appreciation for each subject because of what is revealed ahead. As a caution to parents, there is some "adult language" in the later chapters, but don't let that be the reason your child is kept from reading what is within. For the child that does not learn what is taught ahead, they will be neglected of something they most certainly deserve to know; and the observation of certain language that is used to express sincere emotion is no reason to forego what I assure you is more important than any lesson they will ever attain in any public or private school classroom, or any university course setting, even Ivy League. This book, without question, contains some of the most important knowledge ever revealed to the people of the earth that is long past due for learning.

This book is also written for the *coincidence theorist,* who has been programmed by the lying liars on the television and in the media, and has learned to believe that the number of "coincidences" presented in the media is the way in which the world operates, which is by "coincidence", which it is not. Take for example the story of Mason Wells, the Mormon missionary who survived the Boston Marathon Bombing, the Paris attack of Friday, November 13, 2015, and the Brussels, Belgium Bombing of March 22, 2016, at least if you believe the long nose lying media. *(As reported from Daily Mail, March 23, 2016)*

This type of detrimental programming and mind control over the gullible masses must be broken, and that is exactly what this book will do for any *coincidence theorist* who reads it. If you're reading this now and identifying as one of the many living and breathing *coincidence theorists*, I assure you that you are being mocked, and it is not beneficial to you, or anyone else, other than the tyrants who are getting away with it. So please, read on, and you will be converted from a *coincidence theorist,* to a much more fulfilling and powerful position, a **truth seeker**, and hopefully in time, a <u>truth speaker</u>. What is ahead, will reward all inquiring minds, this is my guarantee. Thank you, and God bless you.

FOUR

CHAPTER

◄⟨∞⟩►

The Complimentary Ciphers to the English Language

Sumerian & Reverse Sumerian

Before we begin to learn these complimentary ciphers, I want you to know that what you have already uncovered with the four base methods is more than enough to open up doors of understanding about the scripted history we're living out, and going to continue to live out, until the Masonic New World Order is stopped in its tracks. Just those four put you a world ahead of those who have no knowledge of the numbers behind the letters. That said, these additional ciphers we're about to unmask will serve as valuable assets in unraveling the numerical code behind the very well thought out English language, even more deeply. If you have your bachelors in Gematria right now, you're about to earn your masters and your doctorate, so put on your learning cap and let's get to it.

1

The first of the complimentary ciphers we will learn, are Sumerian Gematria and Reverse Sumerian Gematria. These two ciphers pertain to Ordinal and Reverse Ordinal Gematria. Sumerian Gematria is simply multiplying each Ordinal value by 6, and Reverse Sumerian is just the same, but doing so for Reverse Ordinal Gematria. The charts for each method are as follows, starting with Sumerian:

Sumerian: A=6; B=12; C=18; D=24; E=30; F=36; G=42; H=48; I=54 J=60; K=66; L=72; M=78; N=84; O=90; P=96; Q=102; R=108 S=114; T=120; U=126; V=132; W=138; X=144; Y=150; Z=156

With this cipher, many interesting observations open up. For starters, notice G sums to

Think about how the capital G is in the middle of the 'Freemason' logo. Using Reduction Gematria, 'Freemason' sums to 42, as covered. At the same time, D.C. is named after George Washington, the 'Freemason', who also has the 42nd State in order of statehood, Washington State, named in his honor. If you use Sumerian Gematria on the initials D.C., it too sums to 42. D.C. = 24+18 = 42

Notice also how X becomes 144. In the last chapter, we covered how XXX is used to symbolize 666, and how the first 144 decimal points of Pi total 666, as well as 'Mark of the Beast' meaning 666, equates to 144. In a moment you'll learn what is known as "Satanic Gematria", which pays the biggest tribute of all to 666, and in that cipher, the word 'ten', equates to 144. Of course in *Roman Numerals,* X is 10.

Also, as I mentioned earlier, using Ordinal Gematria, 'JFK Assassination' sums to 187, and when you multiply 187 by 6, which is exactly what is done with Sumerian Gematria, that number becomes 1122, very similar to November 22, or 11/22 as we write it in the United States. Of course, JFK was reportedly killed on November 22, 1963. I say reportedly, because the only evidence of his death, is from a film made by Abraham Zapruder, who was a 33rd ° Scottish Rite Freemason, that wasn't clear enough to make out anything until the middle of the 1990s, and again, JFK was killed in the middle of Dealey Plaza, also named after a 33rd ° Scottish Rite Freemason… on 11/22. As I have mentioned, Freemasonry, in high places, is a network operating on deception and lies.

Moving on, as we learned last chapter, 'God' also connects to 156. That is through this same method. Recall, using Ordinal Gematria, God equals 26, and when you multiply 26 by 6, it totals 156. For practice, let's do the math together.

God = 42+90+24 = 156 (The number of a man = 156 (O); Man made in God's image)

On the subject of God, you should also know that the Christian portion of the Holy Bible begins with the 930th chapter, which is Matthew 1. Not by chance, 'Christianity' equates to 930 in Sumerian Gematria. As we decode, let us not forget that Adam, the first man, made on the 6th day, lives to be 930-years-old.

Christianity = 18+48+108+54+114+120+54+6+84+54+120+150 = 930

Something else worth remembering is any word with an Ordinal Gematria of 111, will have a Sumerian Gematria of 666. 'Dollar Sign', 'monetary', and 'New York' are words having these qualities. Keep in mind in regards to 'New York', the September 11 attack happened on the date that leaves 111-days left in the year. You might also recall the New York Mets in the 111th World Series, and losing that World Series on November 1, or 11/1. If you weren't following me back then, I said why in Spring Training of that season the New York Mets would most definitely be in that World Series, we'll get to it later. 'The NBA Finals' is another title that sums to 111 in Ordinal, and 666 in Sumerian.

Now, let's transition to the Reverse Sumerian chart.

Reverse Sumerian: Z=6; Y=12; X=18; W=24; V=30; U=36; T=42; S=48; R=54 Q=60; P=66; O=72; N=78; M=84; L=90; K=96; J=102; I=108 H=114; G=120; F=126; E=132; D=138; C=144; B=150; A=156

In terms of the single letters in the Reverse Sumerian cipher, notice that M equates to 84. This is one of the most significant numbers in the study that we have not learned to appreciate thus far. In Reverse Ordinal, 'Masonry' sums to 84, and something very interesting about the letter M is that every single alphabet that has an M in it uses the letter to begin the word Mason, or Masonry, without exception. Just wait until we get to the McDonald's "Golden Arches", especially what happened to them in 1984!

It is in this same cipher where 'Isopsephy', 'Archons', 'Semitic', 'Ciphers' and 'Genesis' each sum to '666' among other things, including 'fingers'. On the subject of fingers, I am sure you are aware of how the 666 hand sign can be made by touching your pointer finger and thumb to form a circle, and then spacing out the middle finger, ring finger, and pinky finger accordingly. If you try this with your left hand, you should be able to quickly visualize the 666-hand-symbol. This is something you will routinely see entertainers do when they are posing for the camera, and often times, quite purposefully. If you make the hand sign with your right hand, it reads as 666 for the person looking at you. In the chapter on sports rigging, I will talk about a very specific *"fingers incident"*, where Mark Jackson, the former NBA player, now color commentator, talked about Stephen Curry's incredible court vision, which prompted Stephen Curry to make the 666 hand signs at that exact moment, and then put them around his eyes, creating the "666 goggles", right on cue, as the camera then zoomed in on his fingers and face. It was one of those magical scripted sports moments, revealing what is truly going on in these very deceptive and dishonest leagues, at least for those with eyes to see, which are few and far between, but we're going to change that truth seeker.

Fingers = 126+108+78+120+132+54+48 = 666

4

Please pay mind that many people make this hand gesture subconsciously while speaking, and they do not mean anything sinister or secretive by it. Sometimes I ask myself if the current President, Donald Trump, is aware that at nearly every moment he is speaking, he is gesturing this sign. Perhaps he is, but one cannot always be certain. If you have seen the film *Network,* from 1976, actor Ned Beatty has a very powerful scene, where he is talking about how we live in a world that is only about dollars and cents. As he is talking about dollars, he begins to make the 666-hand-gesture. As we just covered, in Sumerian Gematria, 'dollar sign' equates to 666, so we can be certain, this gesture, during this memorable scene, is no coincidence. *"The world is a business Mr. Beale!"* If you have not seen the film, please, make sure you do. It is an eye opener, and should be required viewing, because it spells out the truth of what is taking place in this world, including manufacturing terrorism for agenda, viewer interest, and TV ratings. One of the most remembered lines from the film is, *"First, you've got to get mad!"* And truth seeker, let me tell you, I got real mad on September 11, 2001, knowing I was being lied to and I said then, *"I'm a human being damn it, my life has value!"* Just kidding, that's another line from the same film, but what I did say is, "I'm going to get to the bottom of these lies, and I'm going to make sure the whole world knows." That was the seed of what lead to me making the discoveries about the code behind our language, that I now share with you in this book, which will only become more profound from here.

Coming back to financial terms for a moment, 'Dow Jones' sums to 666 in Reverse Sumerian, and 33 in Reduction. If you were paying attention February 2, 2018, the 33rd day of the year, you'll recall the Dow Jones fell by 666 points on this date, and of course not by

Please see:

February 2, 2018 2:53PM

Dow plunges 666 points in biggest drop since Great Recession

By Kevin Dugan

5

coincidence. Making matters even more interesting, if you write out 'February second', or 'thirty-three', or even 'six-six-six', they each equate to 156 in Ordinal. As you learned, 666 is the number of the beast, 'the number of a man', where the latter phrase sums to 156 in Ordinal as well. Keep in mind that man has 33 vertebrae. By observing such things, you can grow your appreciation for how the ciphers work together, and where their relevance is derived.

Further, on October 20, 2017, it was reported that the U.S. fiscal year deficit had increased to $666-billion. Consider, 'October' sums to 666 in Reverse Sumerian. Consider further, that was a

Please see:

BUSINESS NEWS OCTOBER 20, 2017 11:10 AM/4 MONTHS AGO

U.S fiscal year deficit widens to $666 billion

date with numerology of 47 (10+20+17 = 47), and the words 'banks' and 'beast' have Ordinal Gematria of 47. Again, the number 666 is the number of the 'beast'.

Dow Jones = 138+72+24+102+72+78+132+48 = 666 October = 72+144+42+72+150+132+54 = 666

Before we learn the next complimentary cipher, I want you to know that 'Star Spangled Banner' sums to 1776 using Reverse Sumerian, just like the year of establishment for the United States of America, where 'Star Spangled Banner' is the national anthem for the nation. For the record, the name 'Star Spangled Banner' is incredibly coded in multiple ciphers. If you've ever wondered where a word such as 'spangled' comes from, you'll no longer have such questions. In reduction it sums to '33', and that's just the beginning.

Now next up, we're going to discuss what is known as Francis Bacon Gematria. In this cipher, capital letters matter. The code is as simple as this, 'lowercase a through z' is '1 through 26', and 'Uppercase A through Z 'is '27 through 52'.

Francis Bacon: a=1; b=2; c=3; d=4; e=5; f=6; g=7; h=8; i=9;

6

j=10; k=11; l=12; m=13; n=14; o=15; p=16; q=17; r=18

s=19; t=20; u=21; v=22; w=23; x=24; y=25; z=26

A=27; B=28; C=29; D=30; E=31; F=32; G=33; H=34; I=35 J=36; K=37; L=38; M=39; N=40; O=41; P=42; Q=43; R=44 S=45; T=46; U=47; V=48; W=49; X=50; Y=51; Z=52

Right away, what should stand out to you, is capital G, is 33. Think about the Freemason logo, and the Big G. Again, the Masonic headquarters in D.C., has 33-pillars, each standing 33-feet-tall. As we covered prior, the words 'masonry' and 'secrecy' each sum to '33' as well. The words 'masonry' and 'secrecy' also have Gematria of 39, and you'll notice capital M equates to 39 in this method as well. Consider Freemasonry is based in Kabbalah, and Kabbalah is largely based in the 39-books of the Old Testament.

Something else fun to think about is how a deck of cards has 52 total in a set, with 4 categories of 13-cards. If you write the word 'Game', capitalizing the G, it sums to '52', same as the word 'Card', with the C capitalized.

Card = 29+1+18+4 = 52

Game = 33+1+13+5 = 52

In this method, the word 'God' also equates to 52, like the number of weeks in the year. Recall what we learned about the two Aztec calendars, and how they coordinate every 52-years, a special number we will learn to appreciate in the chapter on Kabbalah.

God = 33+15+4 = 52

Also interesting, if you write 'Humanity', with the H capitalized, it totals 137, the 33rd prime number, corresponding with the Reduction Gematria values of 33 for 'people', 'person' and 'goyim', and also tying in with the 33 vertebrae in our back.

Humanity = 34+21+13+1+20+9+20+25 = 137

Another interesting observation is what happens to U.S.A. in this method.

U.S.A = 47+45+27 = 119

Recall, it was September 11, or 11/9, that reshaped the U.S.A. by the numbers.

Essentially, for this cipher, you're adding +26 to the Ordinal Gematria value for every capital letter in a name, acronym, phrase, or sentence. This simple trick opens up a world of meaningful observations that you will uncover as you work with the code. For another example, let's experiment with America before transitioning to the next cipher.

America = 1+13+5+18+9+3+1 = 50 (Ordinal)

America = 27+13+5+18+9+3+1 = 76 (Francis Bacon)

Think about how America, which now has 50 states and many territories, was established in 1776, or '76, where the number 76 connects to 'symbol' and more in Gematria.

For our next cipher, it is the second variation of the Francis Bacon cipher, which we will refer to as Franc Baconis, what was Francis Bacon's alias. In this cipher, capital and lowercase letters again make all the difference, but the arrangement is slightly different.

Franc Baconis: A=1; a=2; B=3; b=4; C=5; c=6; D=7; d=8; E=9; e=10; F=11; f=12

G=13; g=14; H=15; h=16; I=17; i=18; J=19; j=20; K=21; k=22;

L=23; l=24; M=25; m=26; N=27; n=28; O=29; o=30; P=31; p=32;

Q=33; q=34; R=35; r=36; S=37; s=38; T=39; t=40; U=41; u=42;

V=43; v=44; W=45; w=46; X=47; x=48; Y=49; y=50; Z=51; z=52

Just as the other Francis Bacon cipher opens up many meaningful and related observations, so does this one. Notice G sums to 13 using this format. Out of all the numbers important to Freemasonry, the

8

number 13 is among the tops. Consider the United States of America, established by a network of Freemasons, began with 13-colonies, and on the highly Masonic U.S. flag, there are 13-stripes, and were once 13-stars, where the word 'star' in Reduction equates to 13. Also interesting, is that in the Fibonacci sequence, which we will learn more about next chapter, the number 13 is the 7th Fibonacci number. Again, in Ordinal, G is 7.

Of the most important observations in this cipher is the word 'Time'. Using Franc Baconis, the word 'Time' equates to '93', when the 'T' is capitalized, which is another number we have not yet learned to appreciate, but it is one we will discover is of the greatest significance before the end cover. What the number represents is 'Saturn', the sixth planet from the sun, and to the ancients, known as the keeper of time. Until the 1700s, Saturn was considered to be the last planet, and most distant from the earth, prior to the discoveries of Uranus, Neptune, and Pluto, the latter of which, is no longer considered a planet by the majority of science. Equally as important, we are told the sun is 93-million miles away, the true keeper of time.

Time = 39+18+26+10 = 93 (Franc Baconis); Time = 24+23+21+25 = 93 (ALK Kabbalah)

Saturn = 19+1+20+21+18+14 = 93 (Ordinal)

Father Time = 3+8+7+1+22+9+7+9+5+22 = 93 (Reverse Reduction, E22)

In the chapter on September 11, we will uncover how the '93 WTC bombing, blamed on the 'Blind Sheik', a name summing to 93 in Ordinal Gematria, was purposefully coordinated with September 11, 2001, proving that both rituals were not the work of the terrorist boogiemen contrived for news media, but the same New World Order tyrants who are very, very repetitive in how they operate.

Next up, we are going to unlock what is known as Jewish Gematria, a tribute to the numerical coding behind the Latin alphabet, which

9

again, English is based in. If you were not aware, the Latin alphabet, at the time of the fall of Rome, was 23-letters, missing the equivalent of J, U and W. *Sound out those letters.* Now with that said, let's introduce Jewish Gematria, which is also similar to Hebrew Traditional, as we covered in the beginning of Chapter 2.

Jewish Gematria: A=1; B=2; C=3; D=4; E=5; F=6; G=7; H=8; I=9

J=600; K=10; L=20; M=30; N=40; O=50; P=60; Q=70; R=80; S=90 T=100; U=200; V=700; W=900; X=300; Y=400; Z=500

As absurd as this cipher might look, it is full of meaning, and possibly the most relevant of the ciphers you will learn in this chapter. As was mentioned last chapter, the word 'Masonic' sums to 223 in this cipher, a number and relationship worth memorizing. Again, 223 is the 48th prime number, and in both Hebrew and in English, Freemason sums to 48. In English, the word Illuminati also equates to 48, and 223 and 48 are numbers we will come across routinely as we progress. Where the significance of 223 originates, is a Saros, a measurement for predicting eclipses and how modern science is able to be so accurate with such calculations, as each eclipse is working on a perfect pattern, that is 223 synodic months. As mentioned, the mathematics behind the language, are in tribute to the real-world-phenomenon taking place, especially in relation to time. Again, the Freemasons are the masters of knowledge, including that of the sun, moon, stars, spirituality, and most definitely, language.

Masonic = 30+1+90+50+40+9+3 = 223 (The Synagogue of Satan = 223, (O))

In light of the Scottish Rite of Freemasonry being large and in charge when it comes to the code, you'll notice Mc is a very common start to surnames for those of Scottish ancestry. Using this cipher, Mc is 30+3 = 33. *Go figure!* On a related note, in Reduction Gematria, 'ancestry' also sums to 33. As we'll get to, it is the Scottish Rite of Freemasonry in control of police, throughout the United States of America, and much of the modern world. In Jewish Gematria, the word 'police' sums to 147, a number special to Freemasonry, as we began to learn last chapter, and in Reduction, 'police' is 33.

Police = 60+50+20+9+3+5 = 147

Another number worth recognizing from this cipher is 118, representing the word death. On February 15, 2016, I uploaded a video to YouTube, telling Prince, the musician, that I hope he found my video, and he better watch his behind, or he was going to end up dead like his ex-girlfriend, who had been reported dead earlier that day, before the 58th Grammy's *(Purple Rain = 58, Reduction)*. In the video I explained how the numbers 118 and 67 were coded on him, both fateful and both connected to ritualistic killing, as you will learn in the chapter on *Murder by Numbers*, the name of a song by *The Police*, from 1983, where in the lyrics, they teach you that killing is as simple as learning your ABCs. Even better, there's another band called *Slipknot*, and they have a track called *Gematria the Killing Name*. Regarding Prince, to make a long story short, he was found dead 67-days later, 67-days from the death of Vanity, April 21, in the 'elevator' of his home.

Death = 4+5+1+100+8 = 118 (Jewish)

Elevator = 22+15+22+5+26+7+12+9 = 118 (Reverse Ordinal)

Prince = 7+9+9+5+3+5 = 38

Rogers = 9+6+7+5+9+10 = 46

Nelson = 5+5+3+10+6+5 = 34

Prince Rogers Nelson = 118 (Reduction, S10)

FYI, his birthday was June 7, which he died 47-days short of, the number representing 'time' in Ordinal. Think about Prince and the 'Time'. Prince's first album was *For You*, and on his best selling album, *Purple Rain*, a hit song recorded in 1983, 33-years before his death, that is well remembered, goes, "I would die for you", but if you look at the way the track is spelled, it is *"I Would Die 4U"*. Consider that U is the 21st letter, and Prince was found dead April 21, or 4/21, a lot like

'4U', and similar to *'For You'*, his first album. There's a lot more to the story we'll get to in due time.

This same cipher will blow you away when it comes to September 11, 2001. I'm going to save some goodies for the chapter on the subject, but I'll give you a big chunk of meat right now. The Jewish holy day of remembrance for the destruction of the two temples, Solomon's and Herod's, which supposedly were both destroyed on the same day of the Jewish calendar year, 657-years-apart, is known as Tisha B'Av. Using this cipher, 'Tisha B'Av' sums to 911, very similar to how we express the date in the United States, 9/11. For your history bank, the Babylonians in 587 BCE sacked Solomon's Temple, and the Romans destroyed Herod's Temple in 70 CE, after the "Jewish Rebellion" of 66 CE. In both instances, all those years apart, the Temple's were destroyed on what is known as the 9th of Av. For a bit more history, it was 1968, 33-years before September 11, 2001, that 9-1-1 was made the national emergency dialing code, WTC construction began, and George W. Bush, graduated from Yale's Skull and Bones. Not by chance, Bush II has birth numerology of 33, and the title 'Bonesmen', a name given to Yale's Skull and Bones alumni, equates to 33 in Reduction. Let us not forget that in 2004, when he was running for re-election as President, his opposition was John Kerry, who was also part of Skull and Bones, the society only allowing fifteen new members per year, highly exclusive. It was Tim Russert of *NBC's Meet the Press* who exposed this fact and who died later in history "by the code", we'll get to it. Now, let us decode 'Tisha B'Av'.

Tisha B'Av = 100+9+90+8+1+2+1+700 = 911

If you want to get ahead of the curve, try 'al-Qaeda terrorist attack' using this same cipher. I bet you can take an educated guess at what number it sums to. I'll give you a hint; it's the same as 'Jihadists', and 'division'. Also important, the 9th of Av is the 9th day of the 5th month, which is expressed commonly as 5/9, something like 59. In Jewish Gematria, the word 'kill' equates to 59, and this is one to remember, because a lot of people have been 86'd by this exact number, especially those of darker complexions, and we'll cover why in the race war chapter. This also ties in with the two temples being destroyed on this date in history.

Kill = 10+9+20+20 = 59 (59 is the 17th prime) (Kill = 17, Reduction)

Another one of the most important values from this cipher is the output of 144 for the word 'time'. Think about this number in regards to the way we measure time. Each day, has 1,440 minutes (24-hours x 60-minutes). Further, the square root of 144 is 12, something like 12-months in a year, and 12-hours in the AM and PM. In addition to 'time' summing to 144, so does the word 'light', as well as the word 'Nadis', which are important to Hinduism, and measured in quantities of 72,000, as well as 144,000, like the *Tribes of Israel* from *Revelation*, which are also 144,000 in number.

Time = 100+9+30+5 = 144

Light = 20+9+7+8+100 = 144

Nadis = 40+1+4+9+90 = 144

Something else you must know is 'Star Spangled Banner' equates to 666 in this cipher. Making this all the more fascinating is that if you use the four base ciphers, 'Star Spangled Banner' sums to 73 in Reduction, 107 in Reverse Reduction, 190 in Ordinal, and 296 in Reverse Ordinal. Then if you add those four values, 73+107+190+296, the outcome is 666. When you factor in the July 4 birthday of the United States of America, or 4/7, not too far off from 47, the number symbolizing 'beast', things become all the more interesting.

Another important point to know about the 'United States of America', in light of Jewish Gematria, is that the name of the nation sums to 929 in this cipher, matching the number of chapters in the Old Testament. Consider, in Reduction Gematria, 'United States' and 'Old Testament' both equate to 40 as well. It is riddles such as this that prove beyond a shadow of a doubt what group of people truly established this nation, and by what code. Of course, that code is of letter and numbers, and being derived from Kabbalah, as we learned, which is of extreme importance to Freemasonry.

For one last example of Jewish Gematria, and to further the point I just made, notice that the word 'Garden' sums to 137 using the cipher. Consider the *Bible* begins in the Garden of Eden, a story from '*Genesis*', summing to 33 in Reduction, which means 'In the beginning', summing to 137 in Ordinal, where 137 is the 33rd prime number. As we decode, keep in mind the source code of this numerical language behind English is no doubt the *Torah,* which begins with *Genesis,* and in Hebrew, 'Kabbalah' sums to 137, where the knowledge was derived from to construct the *Torah* as it is written.

Garden = 7+1+80+4+5+40 = 137

Next up is what is known as English Extended Gematria. This cipher is a direct tribute to Hebrew Traditional and Greek Traditional and bares much fruit. In the chapter ahead on the Greeks, I will introduce you to their alphabet and coding system, which is very similar to the Hebrew system we acquainted ourselves with in the second chapter. The chart for English Extended Gematria is as follows:

English Extended: A=1; B=2; C=3; D=4; E=5; F=6; G=7; H=8: I=9

J=10; K=20; L=30; M=40; N=50: O=60: P=70; Q=80; R=90 S=100; T=200; U=300; V=400; W=500; X=600; Y=700; Z=800

This is the same cipher 'religion' equates to 260 in. Also related, as we covered last chapter, 666 is a biblical number, and again this code of letters and numbers is absolutely biblical in itself. One more time, it is Johan Gutenberg credited with the first published *Bible.* Let's now decode the name 'Gutenberg' for another 666 to add to the collection.

Gutenberg = 7+300+200+5+50+2+5+90+7 = 666

The word 'business' also sums to 666, and as we know, religion is big business. I just mentioned the scene from the film *Network,* where Ned Beatty's character is signing 666 with his fingers while talking about dollars and the world being a business. Let us not forget we just uncovered how 'dollar sign' equates to 666 as well.

Business = 2+300+100+9+50+5+100+100 = 666

In recent history, we saw Mr. Chicago, Mr. "Sex Sells", Hugh Hefner, die at age 91, on September 27, 2017, what was the Jesuit Order's birthday, an order established September 27, 1540, a date with numerology of 91. Picture him in his red and black smoking jacket. Those colors are the same as the Jesuit's. Chicago, where he called home, a city with major Masonic, Jesuit and Zionist affiliations, only to be outdone by New York in the United States, is one having 91 Gematria in this cipher as well. On the same day he died at 91, the Chicago Cubs clinched their division with their 91st win, what is the 13th triangular number; all part of the script, more in sync than a '90s boy-band.

Chicago = 3+8+9+3+1+7+60 = 91

For some extra calculating practice with this cipher, the word 'religion' sums to 260, as mentioned. As we covered, the number 260 matches the number of chapters in the New

Testament, as we learned in the opening chapter, discussing the significance of the 26-letters in the English alphabet, and the roots of the code.

Religion = 90+5+30+9+7+9+60+50 = 260

Also of significance, the word 'time' in this cipher sums to 254, and September 11, in non-leap-years, is the 254th day of the year. This is a number that shows up again and again in false flag rituals. As mentioned multiple times already, the code largely points back to time, so the numbers relating to time behind the alphabet, are of great importance.

Time = 200+9+40+5 = 254

Light = 30+9+7+8+200 = 254 (Think about 'time' and 'light')

In Ordinal Gematria, 'Saturn, the keeper of time', which is what the planet is known as to the occult, also equates to 254. Recall, you just learned Saturn sums to 93, and again, as we'll get to, the '93 WTC bombing was perfectly coordinated with September 11, 2001.

Saturn = 19+1+20+21+18+14 = 93

The = 20+8+5 = 33; Keeper = 11+5+5+16+5+18 = 60

Of = 15+6 = 21; Time = 20+9+13+5 = 47

Saturn, the Keeper of Time = 254 (Ordinal)

Another good decode in this cipher, is the word 'God'. In Ordinal, 'Zeus' sums to 71, and in English Extend, 'God' does too. At the same time, in Reduction, God totals 17, the reflection of 71. Remember, this cipher pays tribute to the Greeks.

God = 7+60+4 = 71 (English Extended)

Zeus = 26+5+21+19 = 71 (Ordinal)

To build on our appreciation of how these ciphers work together, I want to show you what I call the "Ohio State Buckeyes example". If you're not aware, the Ohio State Buckeyes are the college known for their athletics. Ohio is also known as the Buckeye State. We'll begin by decoding 'Ohio State' with the English Extended cipher, then decode 'Ohio' with Jewish Gematria, followed by 'Buckeyes' with Francis Bacon, followed by 'Buckeye' with Reverse Ordinal, keeping in mind that the number 643 is the 117th prime. We'll also examine 'The Godfather' in Ordinal, the nickname of LeBron James, the Ohio native, and star basketball player of the Cleveland Cavaliers.

Ohio State = 60+8+9+60+100+200+1+200+5 = 643 (643 is the 117th prime number)

Ohio = 50+8+9+50 = 117 (Jewish Gematria)

Buckeyes = 28+21+3+11+5+25+5+19 = 117 (Francis Bacon)

Buckeye = 25+6+24+16+22+2+22 = 117 (Reverse Ordinal)

* The Godfather = 20+8+5+7+15+4+6+1+20+8+5+18 = 117 (Ordinal)

Now let's transition to Satanic Gematria, and I don't mean to scare you away with the name. It is titled this for a very specific reason, paying tribute to 666, the number of the beast. Satanic Gematria is almost the same as the Ordinal Gematria, but instead of starting with 1 and counting up to 26, you begin with 36 and count up to 61.

Satanic: A=36; B=37; C=38; D=39; E=40; F=41; G=42; H=43; I=44;

J=45; K=46; L=47; M=48; N=49; O=50: P=51; Q=52; R=53 S=54; T=55; U=56; V=57; W=58; X=59; Y=60; Z=61

Notice right away, G equates to 42 in this cipher, just as it does in Sumerian Gematria. One more time, 'Freemason' equates to 42 in the Reduction method, and the Freemason logo showcases the G right in the center. But more important than that, is what happens when you write out 'Satanic Gematria' using this cipher. Before decoding, and on the subject of 42 and 'Freemason', you should know that if you take the numbers dividing into 42, and add them together, they sum to 96 (1+2+3+6+7+14+21+42 = 96). Using Ordinal Gematria, the words 'Freemason' and 'Satanic' each equate to 96 as well and using Jewish Gematria, which we just learned, the word 'Free' alone is also 96. Now those points aside, let's decipher 'Satanic Gematria' using the Satanic Gematria cipher.

Satanic = 54+36+55+36+49+44+38 = 312

Gematria = 42+40+48+36+55+53+44+36 = 354

Satanic Gematria = 666

As we covered, the number 666 is the 36th triangular number, meaning if you add the numbers 1 through 36 together, they total 666. Here in this cipher, A is 36. Also, the biggest number in the cipher is Z, what is number 61. One more time, the number 61 is the 18th prime number, and 18 factors into 6+6+6. Ask yourself, could it be anymore perfect? If you write out 'sixty-six-books', it also sums to 666 in this same cipher, what is the length of most Bibles. Equally as interesting, 'first five books' sums to 666, which are in reference to the *Torah*, where the Kabbalah code originates, that brings the relevance to letters, numbers and their respective coding. Personally, observing this, it makes me think that the reason 26-letters was chosen for the English Alphabet, was for this exact reason, to make these calculations possible. Consider, in the *Bible*, a book of coded numbers; it is 666 that is put in the reader's face, in the 66th book, and has been made infamous because of the mystery and intrigue surrounding it.

In this same cipher, please know 'time' sums to 187, a number that is large and in charge, as we covered. It represents Elohim, as well as the beginning and the end, what is time. When we get to our chapter on ritualistic killing, we'll discover how this same number has marked the end of many people's time, if you dig what I'm saying. Also worth mentioning is that Donald Trump had his GOP Convention in 'Ohio', a span of 187-days from Inauguration Day, in "187-Land", 'Washington D.C.'.

Time = 55+44+48+40 = 187

Ohio = 50+43+44+50 = 187

Another important value to remember from Satanic Gematria is that 'death' equates to 213 in this cipher, which we will learn is found around ritualistic killing, time and time again. Tupac Shakur is possibly the best example in the history books of this pattern, but only one of many. In his case, he released his last studio album while alive, *All Eyez On Me,* February 13, 2/13 as it is written in the United States, and then he passed away September 13, exactly 213-days later. Keep in mind February is 'Black History Month', and using Ordinal, the name sums to 213 too. He was also killed due to complications from a 'drive by shooting', summing to 213 in Reverse Ordinal. Even better, if you have seen the film that shares the title *All Eyez On Me,* it begins with his

18

mother, the 'Black Panther', a name that equates to 213 in Reverse Ordinal, and not by accident.

Death = 39+40+36+55+43 = 213

As was mentioned earlier, Holy Bible also sums to 405 in this cipher, not too far off from the Gematria of 45, which Holy Bible equates to in Reduction and Reverse Reduction. Don't forget the riddles with this number and Gutenberg, as well as King James either. And just for good measure, 'Shakespeare' sums to 405 in the English Extended cipher which we just learned. Also in Satanic, it is this cipher where 'Catholic' sums to 351, the 26th triangular number. What I want you to grasp is all of these coding systems are interrelated, and when you work with them, you see just how remarkable they are; it is awe inspiring, and the product of thousands of years of application, predating the existence of English. By the way, please use the website *Gematrinator.com*, where you can load up all of these ciphers at once, type in a word, and instantly compute all values.

Now, let us transition to the next two ciphers, which I will teach at once. They are known as Septenary Gematria, and Chaldean Gematria, and have many parallels.

Septenary: A=1; B=2; C=3; D=4; E=5; F=6; G=7; H=6; I=5; J=4; K=3; L=2; M=1 N=1; O=2; P=3; Q=4; R=5; S=6; T=7; U=6; V=5; W=4; X=3; Y=2; Z=1

Chaldean: A=1; B=2; C=3; D=4; E=5; F=8; G=3; H=5; I=1; J=1; K=2; L=3; M=4 N=5; O=7; P=8; Q=1; R=2; S=3; T=4; U=6; V=6; W=6; X=5; Y=1; Z=7

What I can tell you about these ciphers is quite frequently, a given word will equate to the exact same values in both ciphers, as different as they might appear. I have only been working with these ciphers for less than a year's time at the writing of this book, but again and again, the numbers they generate, are so pertinent to the topic I am often researching. For example, in Chapter 2 we learned how "47" was a very special number to Washington D.C., easily the most relevant number to the city, out of all numbers. By no surprise, using both Septenary and Chaldean, 'Washington D.C.' equates to 47.

Washington D.C. = 4+1+6+6+5+1+7+7+2+1+4+3 = 47 (Septenary)

Washington D.C. = 6+1+3+5+1+5+3+4+7+5+4+3 = 47 (Chaldean)

On a related note, knowing that there are 47 degrees on the Freemasons compasses, and the Masonic headquarters, the House of the Temple, is located in D.C., it is important to mention that many former members of Freemasonry, who have climbed to the highest ranks, have discovered that in the upper echelons, the fraternity is completely satanic, and quickly aborted ship. Using both methods, 'Satanic Temple' also equates to 47. In the Ordinal cipher, the word 'beast' also sums to 47. *Here is wisdom.*

Satanic Temple = 6+1+7+1+1+5+3+7+5+1+3+2+5 = 47 (Septenary)

Satanic Temple = 3+1+4+1+5+1+3+4+5+4+8+3+5 = 47 (Chaldean)

When we get to the chapter on weather warfare by the numbers, we will talk about the flooding of Houston, Texas, on the most appropriate day of the calendar year for such an event, August 27, the 239th day of the year, what is the 52nd prime number. In Ordinal Gematria, 'flood' sums to 52, and August 27, 2017, the date Houston flooded, was a date with 52 numerology to boot (8/27/17 = 8+27+17 = 52); and as mentioned earlier, it was the date Stevie Ray Vaughan had died 27-years earlier, remembered for the album *Texas Flood*. If you look up what was reported in the news, they say 52" of rain fell on Texas in a matter of days, and one more time, weather warfare has been admitted by world militaries since the year 1952. Using the Septenary method, 'Houston, Texas' also equates to 52, a hard thing to call coincidence.

Again, my advice is to use *Gematrinator.com,* free of charge, as you decode history, and you will see how often these two ciphers come into play. Of the two, it seems Septenary is most relevant, but neither should be discounted. Septenary is also the method where 'Saturn' equates to 26, the number symbolizing 'God', and being a number of extreme importance in the *Old Testament,* where Saturn is God. To further establish how the complimentary ciphers are interrelated, and supportive of the base ciphers, let us do a little bit more decoding on Saturn using

Please see:

The Prayer of the Kabbalist: The 42-Letter of Name of God

Book by Yehuda Berg

Septenary and Chaldean. As we decipher, keep in mind Kabbalists have a 42-letter name for God that is in tribute to Saturn, which rules over the heavens, or what we also call outer space.

Saturn = 6+1+7+6+5+1 = 26 (Septenary)

Space = 10+7+1+3+5 = 26 (Reduction, S10)

Twenty-Six = 2+5+5+5+2+7+1+9+6 = 42 (Reduction)

Saturn = 8+8+7+6+9+4 = 42 (Reverse Reduction)

Outer Space = 6+3+2+5+9+1+7+1+3+5 = 42 (Reduction)

Saturn = 1+1+2+3+9+5 = 21 (Reduction)

Saturn = 3+1+4+6+2+5 = 21 (Chaldean)

Twenty-One = 2+5+5+5+2+7+6+5+5 = 42 (Reduction)

Twenty-One = 4+6+5+5+4+1+7+5+5 = 42 (Chaldean)

*21 is the 6th triangular number, and Saturn is the 6th planet from the sun

Freemason = 6+9+5+5+4+1+1+6+5 = 42 (Reduction) (Freemasonry and Kabbalah…)

*Saturn = 19+1+20+21+18+14 = 93 (Ordinal) (903, the 42nd Triangular number)

For another related example of how Septenary compliments the base ciphers, notice how 'sun' equates to 13 using the method, whereas 'star' sums to 13 in Reduction. Of course, the sun is the nearest star that in astrology is tracked in regards to which of the 12 zodiacs it rises in at the vernal equinox, thus 12 zodiac constellations + 1 sun = 13.

Sun = 6+6+1 = 13 (Septenary); Star = 1+2+1+9 = 13 (Reduction)

Space = 8+11+26+24+22 = 91 (Reverse Ordinal) (91, the 13th triangular number)

* Thirteen = 7+6+5+5+7+5+5+1 = 41 (Septenary) (41, the 13th prime number)

And for one last example, notice how 'Outer Space' in Chaldean coincides with 'space' in Ordinal Gematria. As we decode the 44 values, keep in mind 'spiritual' has Reduction Gematria of 44, and 'faith' has Ordinal Gematria of 44. This matters because as we will cover ahead, the original spiritualties of this world, were based in what was taking place above, in the heavens, in the stars. *Think Jesus (the son) and his 12-disciples…*

Outer Space = 7+6+4+5+2+3+8+1+3+5 = 44 (Chaldean)

Space = 19+16+1+3+5 = 44 (Ordinal)

Constellation = 3+2+1+6+7+5+2+2+1+7+5+2+1 = 44 (Septenary)

For three more complimentary ciphers, I will give you a trifecta that are all related as well, and typically used by those studying Kabbalah within the English language. The three ciphers are as follows:

ALW Kabbalah: A=1; B=20; C=13; D=6; E=25; F=18; G=11; H=4; I=23 J=16; K=9; L=2; M=21; N=14; O=7; P=26; Q=19; R=12 S=5; T=24; U=17; V=10; W=3; X=22; Y=15: Z=8

What this cipher is doing is counting every 11-letters, while circling around the alphabet. Notice A is 1, then L, 11-letters after, is 2, then W, 11-letters after, is 3, then if you count from W, it goes X, 1, Y, 2, Z, 3, A, 4, B, 5, C, 6, D, 7, E, 8, F, 9, G, 10, H, 11. Because H is 11-letters later, it then becomes 4, then 11-letters after that is S, which is 5, and so on until each letter is assigned a numerical value. Please recall from Chapter 2, the word 'Kabbalah' sums to 11 using the Hebrew alphabet and related Reduction Gematria system. In the next chapter, you will learn what makes number 11 special, the master number, said to be the greatest of all numbers in terms of numerical meaning.

KFW Kabbalah: A=9; B=20; C=13; D=6; E=17; F=2; G=19; H=12; I=23; J=16; K=1; L=18; M=5; N=22; O=15; P=26; Q= 11; R=4; S=21; T=8; U=25; V=10; W=3; X=14; Y=7; Z=24

LCH Kabbalah: A=5; B=20; C=2; D=23; E=13; F=12; G=11; H=3; I=0 J=7; K=17; L=1; M=21; N=24; O=10; P=4;Q=16; R=14 S=15; T=9; U=25; V=22; W=8; X=6; Y=18; Z=19

Out of these three ciphers, ALW is far and away the most relevant, with KFW being second in line. When you write out 'English Alphabet', using the ALW Kabbalah cipher, it sums to 187, like the number of chapters in the Torah, that the Kabbalah code is based in, and again, matching the value of 'Elohim' in Hebrew, what Kabbalah is traditionally studied in. The math for 'English Alphabet' and its far from coincidental value of 187 is as follows:

English = 25+14+11+2+23+5+4 = 84; Alphabet = 1+2+26+4+1+20+25+24 = 103 **English Alphabet = 187** (ALW Kabbalah)

In this cipher, you'll also come across much overlap with ALW and KFW. Here's one of those times, where 'Presidents Day' equates to 187 in both. *Think about what we learned in regards to D.C and 187...* this is how the entire code comes together.

Presidents Day = 26+12+25+5+23+6+25+14+24+5+6+1+15 = 187 (ALW Kabbalah)

Presidents Day = 26+4+17+21+23+6+17+22+8+21+6+9+7 = 187 (KFW Kabbalah)

There are also some very rare exceptions where each of the three ciphers will equate to the same value for a single word. One of those rarities is 'riddle', summing to 74 in each. Considering Jim Carrey introduced this language of 'Gematria' in the film *Batman*, when he was playing the part of the Riddler, it makes this fact all the more fascinating.

Riddle = 12+23+6+6+2+25 = 74 (ALW Kabbalah)

Riddle = 4+23+6+6+18+17 = 74 (KFW Kabbalah)

Riddle = 14+0+23+23+1+13 = 74 (LCH Kabbalah)

Next up is the Prime Numbers cipher. In this cipher, each letter of the alphabet is a prime number, meaning the first 26 prime numbers are captured, A to Z, as follows:

Prime Numbers: A=2; B=3; C=5; D=7; E=11; F=13; G=17; H=19; I=23 J=29; K=31; L=37; M=41; N=43; O=47; P=53; Q=59; R=61 S=67; T=71; U=73; V=79; W=83; X=89; Y=97: Z=101

In this cipher, 'ritual sacrifice' sums to 477.

Ritual Sacrifice = 61+23+71+73+2+37+67+2+5+61+23+13+23+5+11 = 477

Regarding Hugh Hefner, he died on the 477th birthday of the Jesuit Order, as a ritual sacrifice by the numbers, at age 91. Then just four-days later, at the Route 91 Harvest Festival, on October 1, leaving 91-days left in the year, there was a false flag killing ritual in tribute to Yom Kippur, as we briefly mentioned in Chapter 1, and will take apart in depth in the chapter on false flags ahead. Not by chance, this Las Vegas shooting came 477-days from the Orlando, Florida shooting at the Pulse Night Club, on June 12, 2016, which was the worst mass shooting in U.S. history prior to what transpired in Las Vegas more recently. Consider the supposed brother of the supposed shooter in Las

24

Vegas was interviewed in Orlando, the day after the killing, and even better, 'Orlando, Florida' equates to the same thing as 'Jesuit Order' in Ordinal, which is the number 144, our number connected to 'time', and as you will learn, also killing.

To begin that education, Abraham Lincoln, known as Honest Abe, was shot on April 14, or 14/4, not too far off from 144. Fittingly, in Jewish Gematria, the word 'killer' sums to

As they say, *time is a killer*. At the same time, the name 'Abraham' has Ordinal Gematria of 44, and the nickname 'Honest Abe' equates to 44 in Reduction when 's' is counted for 10. That is similar to how 'kill' equates to 44 in Ordinal and 'shooting' sums to 44 in Reduction, same as 'execution'. Even more, when you write out 'forty-four' as a word, it has an Ordinal value of 144. I bring up this example because Honest Abe would die the day after being shot at reportedly 7:22 AM, April 15, 1865. This is fascinating because using the Primes cipher, 'United States of America' sums to 722, and Lincoln was the President who is credited with saving the nation. Further adding to the riddle is the fact that he died on a date with numerology of 84 and 102, which are numbers corresponding with 'United States of America' as follows.

4/15/65 = 4+15+65 = 84 (United States of America = 84, Reduction)

4/15/1865 = 4+15+18+65 = 102 (United States of America = 102, Reduction, S10)

United   States   of   America   =
73+43+23+71+11+7+67+71+2+71+11+67+47+13+2+41+11+61+23 +5+2 = 722 (Primes)

Next up is the Trigonal Numbers cipher. As we learned prior, triangular numbers are those with mathematical relationships in counting. In the case of 91, since we just discussed it, it is the 13th triangular number because if you add 1 through 13, it totals 91 (1+2+3+4+5+6+7+8+9+10+11+12+13 = 91). Thus in this cipher, the 13th letter, which is M, equates to 91. The entire chart is as follows.

25

Trigonal Numbers: A=1; B=3; C=6; D=10; E=15; F=21; G=28; H=36; I=45

J=55; K=66; L=78; M=91; N=105; O=120; P=136; Q=153; R=171 S=190; T=210; U=231; V=253; W=276; X=300; Y=325: Z=351

This is not a cipher you will use very often, but it one to be aware of. I have included it largely so that you can see the first 26 triangular numbers, which are worth knowing. When we talk about the Bible, we will discuss the triangular numbers 153 and 351, among others, as they are extremely important.

Please also pay attention that when you add 1 through 9 together, it sums to 45, which is numerology terms breaks down to 9 (45 is 4+5 is 9). As we have learned, the number 45 is connected to the 'Holy Bible', 'Geometry' and 'Gematriot', the plural of Gematria, what is Geometry within language. In the next chapter, you will learn what makes the number 9 a very special digit. This quality is one of those special attributes.

For our last cipher, and another you will not use very often, we will uncover the Square Numbers cipher. And yes, this is exactly what you are probably imagining, where each letter represents the squared value of the Ordinal value of each letter. The chart follows:

Square Numbers: A=1; B=4; C=9; D=16; E=25; F=36; G=49; H=64; I=81

J=100; K=121; L=144; M=169; N=196; O=225; P=256; Q=289; R=324 S=361; T=400; U=441; V=484; W=529; X=576; Y=625: Z=676

This concludes our chapter on complimentary ciphers. As we advance to the end cover you will notice that the majority of our decoding is done with the four base ciphers we learned in Chapter 2, but when we do use these complimentary ciphers learned in this chapter, I will be certain to point out which method is in use. Please do not feel overwhelmed with the amount of information uncovered thus far. I assure you that with time, you will become familiar with these various methods, and they will become commonplace. And for one last reminder, *Gematrinator.com* is your friend, the website that makes computing letters into numbers a breeze. That same site can also be used to verify all prime number, trigonal number, and square number relationships, plus more.

FIVE

CHAPTER

◄─────────────◄∞►─────────────►

Numbers as Language, 1-10, 11, 22 and Sometimes 33

The occult meaning behind numbers, especially the digits 1 through 9, known as numerology, is credited to Pythagoras of Samos, born in 580 BCE. As mentioned, Pythagoras, the Greek great, who studied in Egypt, is credited with being the "father of mathematics". In his breakthroughs while studying the science of numbers, he developed spiritual beliefs and theories in regards to the properties that each of the first nine digits possess. Each number after that, in his interpretation, was a recreation of the first nine digits. For example, the number 10, which follows 9, in numerology terms, is $1+0 = 1$; thus the number 10 has the same properties as the number 1. Since the time of Pythagoras, other numerologists have recognized the values of the master numbers, 11, 22 and sometimes 33, which we will also discuss in this chapter. It is important to note that much of Pythagoras's teachings have been lost with time, but some are still intact, which we will touch on in the pages ahead. As we examine the digits, we will incorporate and build on our understanding of Gematria, which is Jewish numerology.

Number One (1) and Number Ten (10)

The number 1 is the only number that divides into all other numbers, making it the most special. In this sense, the number 1 is like God, being found in all things. It is often used to symbolize power, leadership and strength. Think about the desire within we people so often to be number 1, especially when we're younger. Growing up you likely recall wanting to be first in line, first to be called on, or wanting the attention of your parents or those seen as authority before that same attention was received by others around you. In other words, being *numero uno* is a common human desire, most of us can relate to.

As for number 10, in numerology terms, again, it is the same as number 1 (10 is 1+0 = 1). What I want to show you now, is the very special relationship between 1 and 10 that goes beyond just the numerology breakdown. To unlock this seemingly magical relationship, we must add the numbers 1 through 10 together; which are the first two numbers having numerology of 1 (the next is 19). Notice when you sum 1 through 10, it totals 55.

1+2+3+4+5+6+7+8+9+10 = 55

The number 55 is the 10th triangular number, meaning that when you sum 1 through 10, it totals 55, as we just did. In numerology terms, number 55 is 5+5 is 10, and 1+0 is 1. Thus, the first 10 digits, when summed, bring us back to number 1, the number that is most important above all. As just mentioned, 1 symbolizes God. With that understood, let us now decode the word God using our four base ciphers that we learned in Chapter 2.

God = 7+15+4 = 26 (O); God = 7+6+4 = 17 (R)

God = 20+12+23 = 55 (RO); God = 2+3+5 = 10 (RR)

In the Reverse Gematria methods God equates to 55 and 10, again, both reducing to number 1. This relationship becomes all the more interesting when we reduce the word 'numerology' using the Reduction method.

Numerology = 5+3+4+5+9+6+3+6+7+7 = 55 (R)

Speaking of numerology, it is said that the King James Version of the Bible is the most numerological in its orientation. Considering features such as the 55 uses of the word 'Heaven' in Revelation for the KJV, the claim is not without substance.

Heaven = 8+5+1+22+5+14 = 55 (O)

King James = 7+9+4+2+8+8+5+4+8 = 55 (RR)

As we just learned, reducing 55 in numerology terms brings us back to 1. Even more interesting, in the Fibonacci sequence, which is part of God's mathematical spiral, known as Phi and the Golden Ratio, the 10th Fibonacci number is 55. And beyond that, the word 'Fibonacci' equates to 55 using Reverse Reduction Gematria. First, we'll examine the Fibonacci sequence, and then we'll decode the word 'Fibonacci', the name of the Italian mathematician born in 1170 CE, who is credited with the discovery of this very important sequence that we will expand on in the chapters ahead.

Fibonacci Sequence: 1, 1, 2, 3, 5, 8, 13, 21, 34, <u>55</u>

If you count the numbers, you'll notice 55 is the 10th in the sequence (make sure you count both 1s, they are the first two digits in the sequence). The way the pattern works is by adding 1+1 = 2, then 1+2 = 3, then 2+3 = 5, then 3+5 = 8, then 5+8 = 13, then 8+13 = 21, then 13+21 = 34, then 21+34 = 55. The next number in the sequence is 89, because 34+55 is 89. After that comes number 144 because 55+89 is 144. What's interesting about 144 being the twelfth number in the Fibonacci sequence is the square root of 144 is number 12. This pattern goes on to infinity. Let us now decode the word Fibonacci using Reverse Reduction Gematria.

Fibonacci = 3+9+7+3+4+8+6+6+9 = 55 (RR)

In the Hollywood film *Pi*, where Kabbalah and Gematria are introduced, so is the Fibonacci sequence. In fact, Miramax, that put out the film, on their own YouTube account, has a short clip of this portion of the film that I recommend you watch, and it is exactly 3 -minutes and 14-seconds long, just like 3.14, for Pi. In the scene shown in the clip, it is an Orthodox Jewish man, a Kabbalist, who learns from the protagonist about the Fibonacci numbers. The Kabbalist's name is Sol Robeson, summing to 55, in our Reverse Reduction cipher. And even better the protagonist's mentor in the same film is Lenny Meyer, which in Reduction, also equates to the number 55.

Sol Robeson = 8+3+6 + 9+3+7+4+8+3+4 = 55 (RR)

Lenny Meyer = 3+5+5+5+7 + 4+5+7+5+9 = 55 (R)

By applying the code, you'll see that the encoding of character names in books and in films, with numbers that correspond to the key elements of the story, is a common practice. It goes to show, the people who are creating the information we are consuming, are very much aware of the code, but they aren't sharing it with us, they're only hiding it under our noses. Perhaps it is because they think they're "number one". As mentioned in the last chapter, many of these people, especially in Hollywood, are part of the Synagogue of Satan, which is a very real thing and not to be taken lightly. Let us close our learning of the number 1, by decoding 'Satan', which will serve as a reminder of the duality within this numerical language, hidden from day one, ever so cleverly. Also, keep in mind the rock star Marilyn Manson's song, "Say 10", where the chorus goes, "You say God, I say Satan". *There can be little doubt he is aware of the code...*

Satan = 19+1+20+1+14 = 55 (O); Satan = 1+1+2+1+5 = 10 (R)

Number Two (2)

32

The next most important digit is number 2. It is the only number that divides into all even numbers. It is the number that symbolizes the duality of this world, from day and night, to hot and cold, to good and bad, to past and present, and so on. On the subject of 'time', I want to revisit something we covered in Chapter 2. Recall, t is the 20th letter, and in numerology terms, 20 reduces to 2. Also, throughout history, the 't', what is a cross, has been used to symbolize the four seasons, which in total, are often recognized in two parts, the warm months, spring and summer and the cold months, fall and winter. Keep in mind the number 4, is the result of adding 2+2.

Time = 2+9+4+5 = 20 (R);

Seasons = 1+5+1+1+6+5+1 = 20 (R);

Cross = 3+9+6+1+1 = 20 (R)

*20 is 2 in numerology terms

In Freemasonry, their most important symbol is based in this same digit, 2. They are the two pillars, Boaz and Jachin, which were once found at the front of Solomon's Temple, prior to the temple being destroyed and the Babylonians dismantling the two enormous pillars and returning them to their own land. These same pillars, as we will learn, are crucial to Kabbalah and it's Tree of Life; again, Freemasonry has its roots in Kabbalah. As for each of the pillars, Boaz represented strength and the sun, and Jachin represented beauty and the moon. Think about the name of the temple they stood before, Solomon's. Sol is a word symbolizing the sun, and Mon is the root of moon. Throughout history, these two objects of the sky, most visible to us from earth, have been used to keep track of time, past and present. Prior to the Gregorian and Julian Calendars, much of the world was on the moon based calendar, which was 13-cyles of 28-days, what is the lunar cycle.

For your information bank, please note that using Ordinal Gematria, 'two' equates to 58, that special number to Freemasonry, as we covered in Chapter 2. If you look back at the Fibonacci sequence you'll notice the first two numbers of that sequence sum to 2 (1+1), and that the sequence's fifth number is 5, and the sixth is 8, not unlike 58.

Two = 20+23+15 = 58 (O)

Number Three (3)

The number 3 is viewed as a spiritual number, representing the Father, the Son and the Holy Spirit. In the third verse of creation, God brought light into the world, the one thing that makes all other things possible. Not coincidentally, both 'three' and light' are perfect matches in all four of our base ciphers. Let us first read the 3rd verse of Genesis, then we will decode the two words, sharing much in common.

Genesis 1:3 New International Version (NIV) And God said, "Let there be light," and there was light.

Three = 2+8+9+5+5 = 29 (R)

Three = 7+1+9+4+4 = 25 (RR)

Three = 20+8+18+5+5 = 56 (O)

Three = 7+19+9+22+22 = 79 (RO)

Light = 3+9+7+8+2 = 29 (R)

Light = 6+9+2+1+7 = 25 (RR)

Light = 12+9+7+8+20 = 56 (O)

Light = 15+18+20+19+7 = 79 (RO)

Consider, Freemasonry is fixated on the number 33, which is really just the first repdigit of the number 3, where the true significance of 33 resides. As mentioned, the entire code comes back to time, and time can be broken into three parts, past, present, and future. As you learned last chapter, using the Jewish Gematria and English Extended Gematria ciphers, both the words 'time' and 'light' are perfect matches, and having a natural relationship through the sun and moon, which are both objects of light and time. The third object of time, is Saturn.

Also worth recognizing, the number 3 is spelled 'three', having 5-letters. In the case of the first two numbers, 'one' and 'two', they're each three letters long, so why not make the number 3, 'three' letters as well? Before answering that, first recognize that 'light' was created on the 1st day of creation, establishing a relationship between 1 and 3.

Second, the number 3, is the 2nd prime number, thus there is a relationship between numbers 3 and 2 as well. Then third, the number 5 is the 3rd prime number, which brings us to the word 'religion', as well as the word 'Catholic' and also the name 'Elohim', the name of God in *Genesis 1:1*. Let us now calculate each, using Reduction Gematria.

Religion = 9+5+3+9+7+9+6+5 = 53 (R)

Catholic = 3+1+2+8+6+3+9+3 = 35 (R)

Elohim = 5+3+6+8+9+4 = 35 (R); *Creator = 3+9+5+1+2+6+9 = 35 (R)

Let us also examine the word 'eye' using the Ordinal method. You'll notice the word breaks down to 5+25+5, where 25 has a square root of 5. Thus the 3-letter word pays much respect to the two specific numbers, 3 and 5, sharing the prime relationship. As we decode, consider that each human being also has 3-eyes. They are the two on your face, plus the one in your mind, known as the third-eye, or the pineal gland. And on the subject of the mind's eye and the Catholic Church, consider the Vatican has a giant statue of a pinecone, which is in tribute to the pineal gland, looking very similar in appearance.

*Eye = 5+25+5 = 35 (O)

Understand, nothing is arbitrary about our language, from the numbers counted behind the letters, to the number of letters used to form a word. And again, nearly everything about English is in tribute to what is within the *Holy Bible* as well the mathematics of this world in relation to time. Also, as a reminder, prime number relationships are paramount, thus why 'prime numbers' have Ordinal Gematria of 153, and 'Holy Bible' and 'The Bible' have Reverse Ordinal values to match, same as 'Jesuit Order'. To emphasize the point, let us examine *Genesis 3:5,* which has everything to do with the eyes and God.

Genesis 3:5 New International Version (NIV) *"For God knows that when you eat from it your eyes will be opened, and you will be like God, knowing good and evil."*

Number Four (4)

To Pythagoras, this number symbolized God. Not by coincidence, if you sum 1 through 4, 1+2+3+4, the result is 10, another number relating to God. Let us not forget how we began our learning with the four-letter-name-of-God, YHWH, which begins with the 10th letter of the Hebrew alphabet. Also notice, right away, the word four, is spelled with four letters. In terms of time, the 4th astrological sign is 'Cancer', where in Ordinal Gematria, it equates to 44, just the same as 'clock'.

Cancer = 3+1+14+3+5+18 = 44 (O); Clock = 3+12+15+3+11 = 44 (O)

Think about the four seasons of time, and the cross, as we covered. Also, as mentioned earlier, the 4th book of the *Bible,* a text in tune with the stars above, is titled *Numbers*, a major clue to the reader that numbers are of great importance, crucial in one's understanding of this world. The reason the significance of *Numbers* never dawns on so many *Bible* thumpers, is because they are believers, and not thinkers, and because the many Masonic men who are in control of the churches, are not really in their positions to serve God, but instead to hold sway over the people, and to benefit from the collection plate. And please, don't shoot the messenger; I'm just speaking facts.

Back to Pythagoras, the credited "father" of this research, even though it truly predates him by thousands of years; let us now take a moment to decode his name, as well as the word 'mathematics', for yet another parallel to the number 4.

Pythagoras = 7+7+2+8+1+7+6+9+1+1 = 49 (R)

Pythagoras = 7+7+2+8+1+7+6+9+1+10 = 58 (R, S10) (*Born in 580 BCE)

Pythagoras = 3+2+7+6+1+7+2+5+1+6 = 40 (Septenary)

Mathematics = 4+1+2+8+5+4+1+2+9+3+1 = 40 (R)

Mathematics = 4+1+2+8+5+4+1+2+9+3+10 = 49 (R, S10)

As you can deduce, each number calculated has a numerology computing to number 4. The number 49 is 4+9 is 13 and 1+3 is 4; 58 is 5+8 is 13 and 1+3 is 4; 40 is 4+0 is 4. How fitting then that we call Pythagoras, the 'father' of 'mathematics'. As you'll recall from Chapter 2, 'father' also has Ordinal Gematria of 58, breaking down to number 4, the number of foundation, symbolizing the bedrock.

On the subject of 'four', we should also discuss the spelling of 'forty-four', a seemingly nonsensical way to spell 'forty', in light of the fact that the word 'four' has a 'u' in it, so does 'fourteen', but not 'forty'. When I was a child, this bothered me and no teacher could explain the answer to why it was the case. As it turns out, the answer is Francis Bacon and the King James Bible, where this is how the number was spelled, and the reason the spelling stuck. As you know, the number 40 is an extremely biblical number, most remembered from the story of the flood, where the rain lasted 40-days and 40-nights. Very quickly, let me show you what happens when you write out 'forty-four', as well as 'April Fourth', what is 4/4, using the Ordinal Gematria cipher.

Forty-Four = 6+15+18+20+25 + 6+15+21+18 = 144 (O)

April Fourth = 1+16+18+9+12 + 6+15+21+18+20+8 = 144 (O)

37

Let me also show you what happens when you write out 'the flood' and '*Old Testament*'.

The Flood = 2+8+5 + 6+3+6+6+4 = 40 (R)

Old Testament = 6+3+4+2+5+1+2+1+4+5+5+2 = 40 (R)

As we learned last chapter, the number 144 symbolizes time, where again, every single day has 1,440 minutes and the square root of 144 is 12, not unlike the hours in the morning and evening, or the number of months in the calendar year. By the way, 12, in numerology terms, breaks down to 3, and the number 12 is divisible by 3 precisely 4 times. As we just covered, the number 3 connects to light, which connects to time, which brings us around full circle, back to number 4.

Number Five (5)

The number 5 is the balance. It represents creation. Take a look at your hands and your 5-fingers on each. Think about them in light of what we learned about the number 1; on your hands there are 5-fingers, and 5-more, thus 10-total, breaking down to 1, given to you by 1 creator. It is these hands that allow us to be creators as well. I'm using my digits at just this moment to make these words take to the page that you are now likely holding as a book, in your own two hands, with your own two sets of 5-fingers. It is creation that makes all things possible, and because of our own anatomy, it is the number 5 that earns the honor of representing this important characteristic.

Five = 6+9+22+5 = 42 (O); Mankind = 5+8+4+7+9+4+5 = 42 (RR)

As we discussed earlier, in Washington D.C., the very numerological land that it is, there is a 555-foot tall Washington Monument, that many historians say is a phallus, and to be more specific, Osiris's phallus, who was murdered by his brother Set, and cut into many pieces, with his penis forever being lost. It is the male penis that makes up half the equation of creation, and it is reported in many scientific journals, the average male unit is 5", not 6", which the extra inch is something many lovely ladies lust for, such as Osiris's wife, who fashioned Osiris a gold one, after reconstructing his body and bringing him back to life, in the wake of his murder, and giving him a brand new sparkling member, which they conceived a child with, Horus, who then avenged his father, defeating Set. This is an Egyptian myth, the most important Egyptian legend of all. If it is new to you, please look it up. Horus symbolizes the sun, and Set symbolizes Saturn, which also symbolizes Satan (we'll get to it). For a little decoding, we'll now decipher 'sun' using Ordinal Gematria, and 'Horus' using Reverse Ordinal.

Sun = 19+21+14 = 54 (O); Horus = 19+12+9+6+8 = 54 (RO)

To take it further, let's decode the word 'love', knowing the 'sun' is 'love', and makes all of creation possible. Please also notice, 'five' is spelled with 4-letters.

Love = 12+15+22+5 = 54 (O); Love = 15+12+5+22 = 54 (RO)

The symmetry of love! To create, we must make love, it is the human way, and it is the only way. Simply put, love is the ultimate principle of creation. Consider, the number 54 is broken into 5 for creation, and 4 for foundation, thus 'love' is the foundation of creation, an intuitive concept. You could also say love is what brings 'new' life into the world and it is hate that destroys it. And appropriately, in Reduction, the word 'new' is composed of all 5s, and not by chance. The math is as follows.

New = 5+5+5 (Reduction) (*3-letters long, each letter breaking down to 5)

To take that thought about 'new', 5+5+5 and 5 being the number of creation further, consider again the Gematria of 'creator', as well as 'Elohim', the name for God, the architect of this world we share, according to *Genesis*. As we decode, keep in mind, the number 5 is the 3rd prime number, and prime number relationships are paramount.

Creator = 3+9+5+1+2+6+9 = 35 (Reduction); Elohim = 5+3+6+8+9+4 = 35 (Reduction)

Also, for the record, the Washington Monument, which is Osiris's phallus, is 555-feet tall, and sits across from the 5-sided Pentagon, that is 5-floors above ground, with a 5-acre court in the middle. *The 5-sided Pentagon is also 77-feet-tall, and in numerology, 77 is 7+7 = 14 and 1+4 = 5.* Further, the Washington Monument has an extra 111-feet below ground, making the entire unit 666-feet tall, a number you know a thing or two about after Chapter 3. Consider, that monument is the symbol of the 'New World Order', equating to 174 in Ordinal Gematria, the same as 'number of the beast'. And with that said, let us now transition to the number 6.

Number Six (6)

We've already learned a great deal about the number 6, the first perfect number. Recall, mankind is made on the 6th day, and made in the image of the Gods, who are seen as perfect. For review, the word 'man' also sums to 28 in Ordinal Gematria, what is the second perfect number following 6. To add to your knowledge bank, notice the overlap with 'man', 'God', and 'Adam', using just our base ciphers.

Man = 4+1+5 = 10 (R)

Man = 5+8+4 = 17 (RR)

Adam = 1+4+1+4 = 10 (R)

Adam = 8+5+8+5 = 26 (RR)

God = 7+6+4 = 17 (R)

God = 2+3+5 = 10 (RR)

God = 7+15+4 = 26 (O)

(Created in 26th verse of *Genesis*)

At the same time, consider God gave mankind 33-vertebrae, that is connected to the spiritual belief of the Kundalini. As we decode, keep in mind the numbers 33 and 42 both have numerology of 6, corresponding with the 6th day.

People = 7+5+6+7+3+5 = 33 (R)

Person = 7+5+9+1+6+5 = 33 (R)

The People = 7+1+4 + 2+4+3+2+6+4 = 33 (RR)

Vertebrae = 4+5+9+2+5+2+9+1+5 = 42 (R)

Mankind = 5+8+4+7+9+4+5 = 42 (RR)

33 is 3+3 = 6

42 is 4+2 = 6

Also noteworthy, Pythagoras had a special belief about the number 6 according to author W. Wynn Westcott, author of *Numbers, Their Occult Power and Mystic Virtues*. This special belief was in relation to 216, a number we have familiarized ourselves with, learning the product of 6x6x6, or 6-cubed, is 216. Westcott states, according to Pythagoras, every 216-years, all things are renewed on earth, all wrongs, made right. In light of the number 216, consider that the 6th planet is Saturn, the keeper of time, and 21 is the 6th triangular number, meaning that if you sum the numbers 1 through 6 together, they equate to 21. Further, in Reduction Gematria, 'Saturn' sums to 21, just the same as 'Bible' and 'Jesuit'; the latter being the Masonic order within the Catholic Church that is well versed in the knowledge of Kabbalah, the occult meaning of numbers, and the heavens above, which according to them, are ruled by Saturn.

Later, we will uncover the relationships between the Holy Bible, the 6-letter planet Saturn, the planet's relationship with Satan, and Satan's foe, Jesus Christ, but for now you should be able to grasp the relevance of 6 and 3, in light of 666, and 216. As will become clear, these numbers share a significant relationship; such as how 666 is the 36th triangular number, and how the word 'six' is composed of 3-letters, pairing nicely with the fact that 6 is the 3rd triangular number. Building on that relationship is the number 9, which is the numerology of 36, 216, and

666, each reducing to 9, the number that is 6 upside down; and reminding what Jimi Hendrix once said, *"if 6 was 9"*.

36 is 3+6 = 9

216 is 2+1+6 = 9

666 is 6+6+6 is 18, 18 is 1+8 = 9

Consider, the words 'knowledge' and 'Freemason' are 9-letters, equating to 42 in Reduction Gematria, and 96 in Ordinal, which are both numbers reducing to 6 in numerology. In the case of 'Freemason', it is also three syllables, which reminds that Freemasonry is about the pursuit of light and spiritual perfection. On the subject of 3, 6 and 9, a famous scientist and inventor, Nikola Tesla, once said, *"If you only knew the magnificence of the 3, 6 and 9, then you would have a key to the universe."* After doing a little research, it appears he was talking about the spiritual beliefs associated with numbers, including Kabbalah and Hermeticism, both of which we will learn more about in the chapters ahead.

Tesla = 100+5+90+20+1 = 216 (Jewish Gematria)

Hermeticism = 8+5+80+30+5+100+9+3+9+90+30 = 369 (Jewish Gematria)

If you do check out the film *Pi,* you'll notice the protagonist of the film is chasing the number 216, which he learns is important to the stock market (think about what you learned in Chapter 4 regarding the 'Dow Jones' and 666), and also Kabbalah.

Number Seven (7)

The number 7 represents divine completion, and its meaning traces to the story of creation from *Genesis*, where God completes the world and then rests on the 7th day. Remember, the *Bible* is truly a story of what is taking place in the Heavens above. In this world, on our current calendar, we observe each week as 7 -days, with each day of the week being named after one the 7-Luminaries, or what are also known as the

42

7-Classical Planets. Those were the Sun (Sunday), the Moon (Monday), Mars (Tuesday), Mercury (Wednesday), Jupiter (Thursday), Venus (Friday), and Saturn (Saturday). Again, Saturn, the 6th planet from the sun, was the most distant to the ancients, and the 7-Luminaries were the objects that could be observed moving in relation to the stars in the sky. The days were named after the planets from the Greek Hellenistic period, using their understanding of astrology, which is still with us today. The Greek names for the 7 Classical Planets were Sun, Moon, Mars (Ares), Mercury (Hermes), Jupiter (Zeus), Venus (Aphrodite) and Saturn (Cronos).

Other relevance of number 7 from this world we share includes the 7-continets and the 7-oceans. As we will learn in Chapter 7, there are 7-base-metals in alchemy, that correspond with each of the 7-Luminaries, and in Hermeticism, there are 7-Great-Principles of Hermes (Thoth), the Greek-Egyptian God of reading, writing, mathematics and thought, among other things. Even better, there are the 7-notes of the heptatonic scale in 'music'. For some decoding practice, decipher 'seven' and 'music' with the four base ciphers; you should notice overlap in three out of four. Also, given the significance of light, it is composed of 7 colors, *ROYGBIV*. In terms of 7 and completeness, the final book of the Bible is Revelation, which is full of number 7 symbolism; including 7-churches, 7-seals, 7-trumpets, 7-angels, a 7-headed-beast, etc. Fittingly, in Reduction Gematria, Revelation sums to '49', what has square root of 7, and in Ordinal, so does 'Lord'. *Ahead, we will uncover the relationship between the 7-seals of Revelation, and the 7-Great-Principles of Hermes.

Revelation = 9+5+4+5+3+1+2+9+6+5 = 49 (R) (49's square root is 7)

Lord = 12+15+18+4 = 49 (O) (Revelation, about the return of the 'Lord)

For one last thought on 7, think about the letter G in the middle of the Freemason logo. The Freemasons pride themselves on being the keepers of knowledge, and in their lodges and libraries, they secure much of the ancient history and understanding of this world we share. Further, G is the letter we begin the name of God with in English, the one who created the world in 7-days, and who is divine, and who is complete. It is also the letter G, that begins the words Geometry, and Gematria, where God is the master mathematician, and it is Gematria, Geometry within language, according to the Kabbalist, that can help connect the mortal soul with The Creator. Personally, I think the Kabbalist is correct about this much, having been aware of this knowledge since 2013, and having much time to observe life while being aware of the code; more on that in Chapter 22.

God = 7+6+4 = 17 (R) (17 is the 7th prime number) (God, creation, 7-days...)

* Secret Society = 8+4+6+9+4+7+8+3+6+9+4+7+2 = 77 (RR)

Number Eight (8)

The most symmetrical of all the numbers, 8 symbolizes the infinite, power, and strength. In Chapter 1 we began with 26 and how it symbolized God, God's creation, and more. That is a number having numerology of 8, where 26 is 2+6 = 8. Think about it. Does God not symbolize the infinite, power and strength? Interestingly, if you write out 'God's Plan', in Ordinal Gematria, it sums to 88, the 'repdigit' number.

God's = 7+15+4+19 = 45; Plan = 16+12+1+14 = 43 **God's Plan = 88** (O)

Of course, God's plan is in relation to time. Many faithful believe that everything that is taking place on this earth, good and evil, is all part of the divine agenda we are living out day by day. With time in mind, if you look at the number 88 carefully, it is made of 4-perfect-circles. Each circle has 360 degrees, thus 4-circles encompasses 1,440 degrees, similar to the amount of minutes in a complete day, 1,440. Consider further, in the film *Back to the Future,* they always time travel at 88 MPH. Playing on this riddle, on June 2, 2017, a date written 2/6, similar to the Ordinal value of God, summing to 26, *Inside Edition* reported that a man who owned a DeLorean, the same model car from the film, was ticketed for traveling at 88 MPH on the California Interstate. Not by chance, 'California' sums to 88 in Ordinal Gematria, the state that is home to Hollywood. As we decode, keep in mind the mainstream media, from ABC, to CBS, to Fox, to CNN, to MSNBC, to TMZ, to Inside Edition, to the rest contrive news in this manner each day. By knowing the code, it becomes clear these networks are all controlled by people who are practitioners of the knowledge, and who mock the unknowing masses with it; but this mocking will only last for so much longer truth seeker. From *Luke 8*, it is written, "For there is nothing hidden that will not be disclosed, and nothing concealed that will not be known or brought out into the open."

California = 3+1+12+9+6+15+18+14+9+1 = 88 (O)

Now, let's delve a bit deeper into 'time' and its relation to 88, since time truly is limitless, the infinite, not unlike a circle. Appropriately, if we write 'three-hundred-sixty', the degrees in one circle, it totals 88 in Reverse Reduction.

Three Hundred Sixty = 7+1+9+4+4+1+6+4+5+9+4+5+8+9+3+7+2 = 88 (RR)

Even better, if we write 'circle' and use the ALW Kabbalah and KFW Kabbalah ciphers, as learned in Chapter 4, they both sum to 88.

Circle = 13+23+12+13+2+25 = 88 (ALW Kabbalah)

Circle = 13+23+4+13+18+17 = 88 (KFW Kabbalah)

So there it is, the number symbolizing the infinite, has a strong relationship with the circle, also symbolizing the infinite. It makes one wonder if it is a coincidence that when Jews immigrated to the United States, they were known for circling the box of their religion, when they were instructed to check the box. In case you didn't know, this is the origin of the term kike, which comes from the Yiddish word kikel, which means 'circle'.

Jewish = 17+22+4+18+8+19 = 88 (RO)

Number Nine (9)

The number 9 represents completion, as it is the last of the single digits. This number has real world significance in the human gestation period, where a typical pregnancy lasts 9-months. Pythagoras was particularly fascinated by this number, comparing it to God, just as he did with the number 4. Recall from the start of the chapter, the name Pythagoras has Gematria of 49, also capturing the two digits of his numerological fascination, 4 & 9. Speaking of which, if you write the number 4 by hand, and the number 9, they are extremely similar in appearance. Also intriguing, is that in Reverse Ordinal Gematria, if you write out 'forty-four', with the mutilated spelling that it purposefully has, it totals 99.

Forty-Four = 21+12+9+7+2+21+12+6+9 = 99 (RO)

In numerology, there are two very unique things about number 9 that are not true for any other number. First, if you add 9 to any number, it will preserve the numerology it had before you added 9. To make the point, if you add 9 to 1, it becomes 10, breaking down to 1. Then if you add 9 to 2, it sums to 11, breaking down to 2. Even more, if you add 9 to 3, it sums to 12, breaking down to 3, and so on. There is no exception to this rule. That is why in our Reduction Gematria ciphers, each letter that is spaced out by 9, breaks down to the same digit. For example, A, the 1st letter, J the 10th letter, and S the 19th letter, each equating back to number 1 in Reduction Gematria, same with B the 2nd letter, K the 11th letter, and T the 20th letter. You might have also noticed that in Reduction and in Reverse Reduction, 'I' and 'R' are the only digits breaking down to 9. The second thing that makes number 9 special is that if you multiply any number by 9, it will take on numerology of 9. Notice the following examples.

46

9x1 = 9

9x2 = 18 (18 is 1+8 is 9)

9x3 = 27 (27 is 2+7 is 9)

9x303 = 2727 = 2727 is 2+7+2+7 is 18; 18 is 1+8 is 9)

Again, there are no exceptions. The other thing cool about 9 involves our hands and multiplication. Put your hands in front of you with your palms facing you. Now put down your left thumb and tell yourself that means 1x9. You'll notice, the fingers left standing, count to 9, what is the product of 1x9. Now, on your same left hand, put your thumb back up, and instead drop your left pointer finger. Tell yourself that means 2x9. If you count your fingers, you have 1 thumb up, then a finger down, and then 8 consecutive fingers up. Imagine the 1 thumb and the 8 fingers up represent 18. Now, put your left ring finger back up, and drop your left middle finger, with this meaning 3x9. If you count your fingers, you have your thumb and pointer up, representing 2, then you have a gap because your middle finger is down, and you have 7 more fingers in a row standing, which represents 27. This is much like 3x9 = 27. You can do the same thing with each finger, getting the correct answer for 9 x the digit number that is down, all the way up to 9x10 = 90. This is something you cannot do with your fingers for any other numbers, and this is another reason why number 9 is so sacred, even godlike.

More on Number Ten (10)

In the beginning, we covered how 10 and 1 are equivalent in numerology terms. Here, I want to provide a few more notes about the number 10 itself. As we learned in the first chapter, in Hebrew, the 4-letter-name-of-God, YHWH, begins with the 10th Hebrew letter, Yod, very similar in spelling and appearance to 'God', which has a Reverse Reduction value of 10. Consider, it is YHWH who provides the 10 Commandments to Moses, which are to help man avoid 'sin'. Fittingly, in Reverse Ordinal, 'ten' sums to 42, and in Ordinal, 'sin' equates to 42 just as well.

As you know, the opposition to God is 'Satan', who seeks to help man fall into sin, having a name summing to 10 as well, in Reduction Gematria. What is fascinating about the Old Testament, which is 39-books in length, corresponding with the Ordinal value of 'ten', summing to 39, is that it makes it unclear who the Lord is. Is it God, or is it Satan? To illustrate this seemingly purposeful confusion within the text, let us examine the verses *2 Samuel 24:1-2*, which is from the 10th book of the *Bible,* and then let us examine *1 Chronicles 21:1-2*, which is from the 13th book.

2 Samuel 24:1-2 (NIV): Again the anger of the Lord burned against Israel, and he incited David against them, saying, "Go and take a census of Israel and Judah." So the king said to Joab and the army commanders with him, "Go throughout the tribes of Israel from Dan to Beersheba and enroll the fighting men, so that I may know how many there are."

1 Chronicles 21:1-2 (NIV): Satan rose up against Israel and incited David to take a census of Israel. So David said to Joab and the commanders of the troops, "Go and count the Israelites from Beersheba to Dan. Then report back to me so that I may know how many there are."

These verses, which are widely studied and debated, should be considered within the context of Gematria. Consider the 'Great War', summing to 39 in Reduction, which began in 1939, emphasis on '39, and where 'war' has an Ordinal value of 42. Was that war for good, or was it for evil? Because its legacy is the nation of Israel, which is now the home of the Synagogue of Satan, the false Jews, as we will elaborate on ahead.

Master Number 11

The number 11 is said to be the most powerful number because it encompasses the digit 1, the only number dividing into all numbers, symbolizing God in doing so, and because it also breaks down to 2, the next most powerful number, only behind number 1. In the *Holy Bible,* the Son of God is said to be 'Jesus', which as we learned, in Reduction, is a name equating to 11, which once again corresponds perfectly with the 66-books of most Bibles. In case you have forgotten, the number 66 is the 11th triangular number, meaning if you add 1 through 11 together, it totals 66. Of course, the 66th and concluding book of the *Bible, Revelation (22 chapters long)* is about the return of Jesus. Also, as we learned, 'resurrection' sums to 66 in the Reduction method, the same way 'Jesus' equates to 11. Further, the story of the resurrection of Jesus Christ (11-letter-name) comes from the 89-chapters of the *Gospel,* where number 89 is the 11th Fibonacci number.

It is said that people who have birth numerology of 11 are natural born leaders. It is a coveted number in this study, and there can be no doubt it is coded into the name Jesus for all that it symbolizes in the language of numerology, the master number. It is the same reason 'Kabbalah' sums to 11 in Hebrew Reduction Gematria, as covered. In terms of English Gematria, the word 'master' also factors into 11. Let's decode and examine.

Master = 4+1+1+2+5+9 = 22 (R); Master = 4+1+10+2+5+9 = 31 (R, S10)

In the case of 'master' summing to 31, when 'S' is observed as 10, 31 is the 11th prime number. Consider 'Gematria' and 'English', each equate to 38 and 74 in Reduction and Ordinal Gematria, numbers breaking down to 11. As for it summing to 22 in regular Reduction, the number 22 is the 'master builder' number, which according to some numerologists is even more powerful than 11, carrying a more magnificent vibration. Let's now transition to 22, which also plays a huge role in the concluding book of the *Bible, Revelation.*

When we get to 9/11 (9+1+1 = 11), we'll talk about Flight AA-11, flying into the 110-story World Trade Centers that appeared as massive

49

11s, in the skyline of the 11th state, 'New York', a state name summing to 111 in Ordinal Gematria. We'll also discuss how that attack was blamed on 'Osama bin Laden', equating to 110 in Ordinal Gematria.

Master Number 22

Revelation is about the return of the 'Lord' Jesus Christ, and it is exactly 22-chapters long. Appropriately, the word 'Lord' in Reduction, equates to 22.

Lord = 3+6+9+4 = 22 (R)

The number 22 is special because it contains the digit 2, which symbolizes duality, as well as coming together and taking apart. Think about how it is called the 'master builder' number. Constructing and deconstructing are foundational concepts to the builder, and since this language is a construct of the Freemasons, who were traditionally builders of the spiritual houses of worship, across all faiths, let's look at the Gematria of the phrase 'master builder'. It has a lot to do with 'Freemason', not by surprise.

Master Builder = 13+1+19+20+5+18+2+21+9+12+4+5+18 = 147 (O)

As you'll recall from our earlier learning, the words 'Freemason' and 'conspiracy' share Reverse Ordinal Gematria of 147. Also, as mentioned, when you write out 'ninety-four' as a word, in Ordinal Gematria, it sums to 147, and Revelation 9:4, not unlike 94, is the 147th verse of the book. Even more, the number 94 in numerology terms breaks down 9+4 is 13 and 1+3 is 4. So does the number 22, the master builder number.

As we learned in Chapter 2, the number 4 represents foundation, and when it comes to building, you always begin with the base, which is why the Freemason's use Euclid's 47th problem as part of their logo, the problem that teaches how to create a perfectly square foundation (4-sides) by using rope, anchor points, and the North Star, or what they refer to as the Polestar, for the sake of its '47' Gematria, as covered. One more time, the number 4 has divisors summing to 7, and 7 is the 4th prime number. The number 22 can also be divided by the number 7 to solve for Pi, as we covered in Chapter 2.

For you sports fans out there, you might be aware that in American football, as well as in soccer, there are 22 -players on the field. As we just learned, when you write out 'master builder', it sums to 147. In the case of American football, from the first Sunday of the NFL season, to Super Bowl Sunday, is exactly 147-days. Also related, in the case of American baseball, the championship is called the 'World Series', despite the sport only having teams from one continent. Not by surprise, 'World Series', using Ordinal Gematria, equates to 147. As for the NBA, the court dimensions are 94'x50', and again, when you write out 'ninety-four' as a word, it sums to 147. In the 2016-17 NBA season, the Warriors defeated the Cavaliers for the fourth time, June 12, 2017, winning the championships, exactly 147-days after blowing out "King James" on Martin Luther King Jr. Day, January 16, 2017. Of course, the words 'basketball' and 'king' sum to 22 in Reduction Gematria and Reverse Reduction Gematria respectively, the 'master builder' number. Related, if you do the math on the dimensions of the NBA court, what is 94'x50', it makes a square footage total of 4,700'. As we learned, the number 47 represents 'foundation', in Reduction Gematria, and is important to the Freemason logo, which was important to James Naismith, the credited pioneer of basketball, who also was a Freemason, same as Walter Camp who created American football, and Abner Doubleday who created American baseball.

Even more interesting, in Genesis 47, Jacob, who becomes Israel, dies at the age of 147. If you write out 'forty-seventh', it too sums to 147 in Reverse Ordinal Gematria. Think about David Stern and Adam Silver, the faces of the recent decades of the NBA, who are both Jewish men, and proud supporters of Israel. Also, the first professional basketball championship in the United States, was played in '47, and won by the team from Philadelphia, the biblical land that it is; the church warned about the Synagogue of Satan in the 22-chapters of Revelation.

Forty-Seventh = 21+12+9+7+2 + 8+22+5+22+13+7+19 = 147 (RO)

And for another crucial example of the number 22 in language, using Reduction Gematria, both the words 'food' and 'water' sum to 22. These are the two things that build and maintain the body, above all. It is said that a person can go 3-days without water, and 3-weeks without food, before perishing. As we decode the words 'water' and 'food', note the 666 found within the letters making up the word 'food'. In *Genesis,* decoding to 666, there are very specific directions from God about what people are to eat, and those foods are fruits, vegetables and seeds. If you are not aware, the human digestive tract is that of an herbivores, nothing like a carnivores and not much like an omnivores either, yet most people have been programmed to eat meat and animal protein through advertising and corporate media, where the "food pyramid" is a construct of big 'business', and not true science. It is scientific fact, that the vegetarian diet is superior, and it is not coincidental that it is commanded as man's diet from the start of 'Genesis'.

Food = 6+6+6+4 = 22 (R); Water = 5+1+2+5+9 = 22 (R)

Master Teacher 33

As we have learned, we human beings have 33 vertebrae in our backs, and the words 'people', 'person' and 'goyim' each equate to 33, as does the word 'teacher' corresponding ever so nicely with the fact it is the 'master teacher' number, just the same way the word 'master' corresponds with 11 and 22. For the record, the word 'student', in Reduction Gematria, sums to 22, and 31 when you take into account S as 10. Think about how the teacher helps build the student, but this can only happen when there is 'order' in the classroom, another word summing to 33 in Reduction Gematria.

Above all, 33 is the number of 'order', and order is something that is natural, like the count of vertebrae making up the human spine, but also something that must be taught with discipline, and rules. In terms of the alphabet, I would like to show you something so very interesting about the first 6 letters, and the final 6 letters, in light of the title, 'alphabetic order'. Keep in mind that the number 33, in numerology, reduces to the number 6. Now, let's decode 'alphabetic order' using our Ordinal cipher to get started.

Alphabetic Order = 1+12+16+8+1+2+5+20+9+3+15+18+4+5+18 = 137

Again, the number 137 is the 33rd prime number. As we learned prior, "In the beginning" sums to 137, and the name *Genesis* sums to 33. As we have also covered, 'Humanity', using the Francis Bacon cipher equates to 137, tying right in with our human anatomy and the ancient spiritual belief of the Kundalini and the 33-vertebrae; a belief incorporated into the Gematria of 'masonry', as well as 'order' and 'secrecy', where all three emphasized words equate to 33 in Reduction. Now to take this a step further, we will decode the first 6-letters of the alphabet, as well as the final 6.

ABCDEF = 8+7+6+5+4+3 = 33 (RR)

ABCDEF = 26+25+24+23+22+21 = 141 (RO)

UVWXYZ = 3+4+5+6+7+8 = 33 (R)

UVWXYZ = 21+22+23+24+25+26 = 141 (O)

Thirty-Three = 7+19+18+9+7+2 + 7+19+9+22+22 = 141 (RO)

Notice how in Reverse Reduction, the final 6-letters sum to 33, and in Reduction, the first 6-letters equate to 33. This is a logical outcome and verifies the symmetry of the alphabet and the coding system. Please also notice how 'thirty-three', when written out as a word, equates to 141, same as the first and final 6-letters (33 is 3+3 is 6).

In the chapters on Masonry and Christianity ahead, you will learn about the relationship between 33 and 74 (11). For now, please know that 'English Language' sums to 74 in Reverse Reduction, and 'Numerical Language' sums to 74 in Reduction. As we covered earlier, 'English' sums to 74 in Ordinal, the same as 'Gematria', 'Masonic' and 'Occult'. When all the pieces of the puzzle are observed and interpreted, there can be no mistaking these synchronicities for "coincidence", a painful word, used to dismiss truth too often.

Let us now conclude our learning of 33 by revisiting its significance to the *Bible,* which begins with *'Genesis',* meaning 'In the beginning'. Of course *Genesis* is a story from where the lessons of life are taught.

Bible = 7+9+7+6+4 = 33 (RR)

Good Book = 2+3+3+5+7+3+3+7 = 33 (RR)

Genesis = 7+5+5+5+1+9+1 = 33 (R)

In the beginning = 9+14+20+8+5+2+5+7+9+14+14+9+14+7 = 137 (O) (137, 33rd prime)

Recall, 'Kabbalah', sums to 137 in Hebrew Gematria.

And in terms of 33 and beginnings, we'll close with the Gematria of 'seed' and 'birth'.

Seed = 19+5+5+4 = 33 (O)

Birth = 7+9+9+7+1 = 33 (RR)

How to Use These Numbers In Relation to Gematria

For the concluding piece, let us now understand how numerical meaning factors into Gematria encoding. As we have gathered, the numbers behind the words are not arbitrary, but are based in the mathematics of this world, and logical relationships with numbers that have real world basis. Thus, when we decode words and find their values, such as "58" for example, we can understand why those numbers are coded into the specific words that they are. In Chapter 2 we learned how 58 pertains to God, the Heavens above, and 'Freemasonry'. The digits that make up that number are 5 and 8, the fifth and sixth Fibonacci numbers. As we learned, number 5 represents creation, and number 8 represents the infinite. Think about God, the infinite creator and the faith of Masons, who are creators in their own right. Think further about space, or the heavens, and their infinites, as well as the fact that they gave birth to us, the children of 'stardust', who will continue to procreate until our nearest star stops shining.

Stardust = 8+7+8+9+5+6+8+7 = 58 (Reverse Reduction)

Further, when you take the numerology of these numbers, they are also relevant. So in the case of 58, it becomes 5+8 is 13 and 1+3 is 4. As we know, number 4 is the foundation. With that in mind, what is more foundational than God, who sports the 4-letter-name, YHWH, which is also known as the 'Tetragrammaton', summing to number 58 in Reduction? The same can be said for space, which contains all things, including us. And as for Freemasonry coding the number on their organization, I think that point can be understood. As the keepers' of knowledge, and the invisible architects of this world we live in, they most certainly see themselves as the foundation of the agenda being pushed forth on this earth, what Manly P. Hall called the Order of the Quest, the goal of establishing a one world government, based in democracy and philosophy.

For more practice, please decode the words 'democracy' and 'philosophy', as well as 'Freemason, and 'Mason' and 'Accepted Scottish Rite of Freemasonry'. You need only use the four base ciphers. Then look at the numbers deciphered, and think about them in light of what you learned in this chapter. What you should take away is numbers are a language unto themselves, and it is this language, older than English, that the words of English have been constructed upon, thus why 'forty' is 'forty' and not what it logically should be *'fourty'*. And remember truth seeker, there is always more.

SIX

CHAPTER

◄∞►

Sacred Geometry, Where Letter, Number, Shape, &
Symbol Meet

Out of all the important shapes and symbols relating to Sacred Geometry it is the Flower of Life that is the most coveted because of how many other relevant geometric shapes it gives birth to, which we will uncover. Every religion of the world pays homage to this shape, without exception. Please take a moment to examine the Flower of Life, shown to the left, knowing it is composed of 61-circles, a very special amount, being the 18th prime number, and where 18 factors into 6+6+6. As we covered in Chapter 3, the number 666 relates to Metatron's Cube, which is also related to the Flower of Life, and is meant to symbolize creation, same as the Flower of Life. It is because of this shape, the Flower, that in Ordinal Gematria, the word 'prime' equates to 61. Just wait until we get to Roger Maris's scripted record

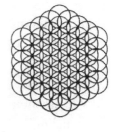

61st homerun in the year '61, recognizing a 'baseball', summing to 18 in Reduction Gematria, is circular, and the Flower of Life is 61-circles. It has been said by others that 'game' is 'God', and the word 'God' sums to 61 in Jewish Gematria, whereas 'game' and 'God' sum to 26 in Ordinal Gematria. It has also been said that the Flower of Life is God.

On the subject of religion and God, take a moment to consider Christianity and the spiritual centerpiece of the faith, Jesus Christ, the Son of God. Here is a short list of words, having Gematria of 61 that pertain to the faith. As we decode, understand that the symbolism within prime numbers is power and strength, because they cannot be divided, they are inseparable, like the Christian who has faith never wavering.

Jesus = 17+22+8+6+8 = 61 (RO)

John = 17+12+19+13 = 61 (RO)

Cross = 24+9+12+8+8 = 61 (RO)

Christian = 6+1+9+9+8+7+9+8+4 = 61 (RR)

Christmas = 6+1+9+9+8+7+5+8+8 = 61 (RR)

Church = 3+8+21+18+3+8 = 61 (O)

Out of the many shapes that can be derived from the Flower of Life, are the 'Fruit' of Life, and 'the Seed of Life'. Not by chance, the word 'Fruit' has Reverse Ordinal Gematria of '61', and so does the entire phrase, 'the Seed of Life' in Reverse Reduction. Consider further, in the story of creation from *Genesis*, God gives mankind fruit and seeds to eat, commanding a vegetarian diet, something that changes later in the *Bible*.

Fruit = 21+9+6+18+7 = 61 (RO)

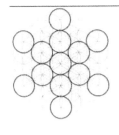

The   Seed   of   Life   =
7+1+4+8+4+4+5+3+3+6+9+3+4 = 61 (RR)

To the left is the Fruit of Life overlaid on the Flower of Life. Notice it is composed of 13-circles, taken directly from the Flower. In terms of Jesus Christ, his initials, JC, in Ordinal, are 10+3, 13, and it is he and his 12 disciples, or 13-men, not unlike the Babylonian Zodiac of 13 constellations, or the current Zodiac, where we observe 12 constellations of stars, plus the sun, the most crucial star of all. This also connects to Revelation 13, where the Isopsephy riddle is presented to the reader about 666, the number of the beast, and the number of a man, who was created on the 6th day of creation. In terms of the earth and its relation to the sun and stars, according to science, the earth is tilted at a 23.4-degree-angle, meaning it is 66.6-degrees off center. Keep in mind we are said to be the children of the stars, the children of earth; *as above, so below.* And let us not forget, 13 is the 6th prime number.

This same shape, the Fruit of Life and its 13-circles, is claimed to be the blueprint of the entire universe, capturing the foundation for the design of the molecular structure of all living organisms. It is also the key geometric shape within the larger Flower of Life for what is Metatron's Cube. And you must know, I am not here to argue the scientific relevance or accuracy of any of this, I am only showing you what is believed, and what is studied, and what is practiced, so that you are no longer in the dark about these beliefs of others, that are influencing all of our lives, Christian or otherwise.

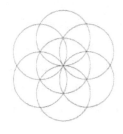

Next up is the Seed of Life, which are the 7-circles from the center of the Fruit of Life that is taken from the center of the Flower of Life. For anyone who has sliced open an apple, or any other fruit, surely you know about the seeds in the center; thus the reason for the name, Seed of Life.

Understand, all these geometric shapes, come from the world around us, from the natural environment God created for us. All of this knowledge is intuitive. Please take a moment to gander at the Seed of Life, shown to the left. Here it is pictured with the 7-circles overlapping, forming multiple Vesica Piscis, or what is known as the womb of the universe, and is yet another symbol that is showcased in all religions of the world.

Again, 7 symbolizes the divine, and to the spiritual, this symbol is a visual representation of how God created the world, using 7-days for the entire process. Using Sacred Geometry, the belief is God began with one sacred circle, which is the circle in the center of the Seed of Life, and each day multiplied from that circle to bring the next component of creation into existence, similar to the way he made Eve from Adam's rib, and similar to how before that, he made Adam from the soil that came before man when the earth was born. In other words, one creation leads to the next.

Now please take a moment to examine the Vesica Piscis shown to the right and think about all the places this shape shows up, from religious symbolism, to the American football, to the human eye, to an almond, to the womb of a woman. Of course it resembles a fish bladder as well, and in Latin, that is exactly what Vesica

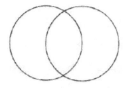

Piscis means, fish's bladder. In Christianity, it is commonly called a 'Mandorla', which has Reduction Gematria of 33, and most often, it is shown around Jesus Christ. On the backs of Christian car bumpers, you'll often see it on its side, in the body of a fish, with the letters IOXYE, or a cross. Of course this symbol also represents Pisces, the Age of the zodiac we are living in, as covered in Chapter 1. You'll also see the same symbol used in mocking fashion on car bumpers, with the word 'Darwin', or 'N'Chips'. For a little practice, decode the words, 'Mandorla', 'IOXYE' 'Darwin', and 'N'Chips', and you will find that they all sum to 33 in Reduction, plus more. In our chapter on scientific history by the numbers, we'll learn that Darwin was both born and dead on a date with numerology of 33, reminding of Jesus, who was crucified at the youthful age of 33.

Now for some more Gematria practice, we will decode the words, 'Fish's bladder', 'Vesica Piscis', 'womb', 'religion' and 'Sheela-na-gigs', where the later are spiritual carvings found across the world, that exaggerate the womb of a woman. We will use our base ciphers, taught in Chapter 2, for this decoding. Again, the Vesica Piscis is said to be the womb of the earth, representing what all of creation is born from, and relating to the Seed of Life, which contains multiple Vesica Piscis. Please also pay mind that the shape is formed by the duplicating and overlapping of two equal circles, which ties in with the belief from the Seed of Life, about how God created the world by forming additional circles, day by day, replicated from the one source circle.

Fish's bladder = 6+9+1+8+1+2+3+1+4+4+5+9 = 53 (R)

Vesica Piscis = 4+5+1+9+3+1 + 7+9+1+3+9+1 = 53 (R)

Vesica Piscis = 5+5+6+5+3+1+3+5+6+3+5+6 = 53 (Septenary)

Womb = 23+15+13+2 = 53 (O)

Sheela-na-gigs = 1+8+5+5+3+1+5+1+7+9+7+1 = 53 (R)

Religion = 9+5+3+9+7+9+6+5 = 53 (R)

In light of the encoding of number 53, as we learned in Chapter 5, the number 5 is the 3rd prime number, and 5 represents creation, where 3 represents spirituality and light, making all things possible. So how appropriate that the shape representing the *womb of the universe* have these specific numbers coded within, in our most relevant cipher? On a related note, we will learn later about the significance of sex in this study, where the womb of a woman and creation goes hand in hand. Also related, using the Ordinal method, 'sexual' sums to 82, and using Reverse Reduction, 'Vesica Piscis' equates to 82. In terms of news by the numbers, in October of 2017, 'Harvey Weinstein', summing to 82 in Reverse Reduction, the famous Hollywood tycoon, received considerable media shaming for reportedly groping a number of very famous women, a story that emerged in the time of Donald Trump, the "groper-in-chief". In the chapter on Trump, we will discuss how these stories were most definitely coordinated, as Hillary Clinton, the opponent of Trump, also became a major part of the story. At the same time as those headlines were taking place, another actress came out and accused another Hollywood type, Ben Afflek, of wrongfully groping her, an actor who had performed in films funded by Weinstein. The actress, who helped take some of the attention off the wrongdoing of Weinstein with the accusations against Afflek, was 'Hilarie Burton', a bizarre spelling for the name that is most commonly Hillary. Using her Hollywood actress's name spelling, the name sums to 82, matching her birth year of '82, as well as the Ordinal breakdown of her initials, where H is 8, and B is 2. Again, every single day, news is manufactured by the code, and this is but one tiny example. You can prove this to yourself by taking the time to look back at your most remembered news stories, and applying the knowledge. You can also quickly find out why your favorite celebrities have had their names modified, as they so often do when they make it to the limelight.

For a bit more on 'the Vesica Piscis', I want to show you how the name brings the crucial concepts of this entire text together. As we will prove, the words 'language', 'mathematics', 'Sacred Geometry', 'Old Testament' and 'planet' are each equating in Gematria terms. Again, this practice of Gematria is in relation to the way God supposedly created the world through language, a belief of Kabbalists. As we are about to discover, all of these emphasized words sums to 68, a number containing 6, representing perfection, and the number 8 representing the infinite. As we have mentioned, mathematics are infinite, they are exact, and they are perfect. Even further, if you breakdown 68 in numerology terms, it is 5, our number of creation. Think about it.

The Vesica Piscis = 2+8+5+4+5+1+9+3+1+7+9+1+3+9+1 = 68 (R)

Sacred Geometry = 1+1+3+9+5+4 + 7+5+6+4+5+2+9+7 = 68 (R)

Mathematics = 5+8+7+1+4+5+8+7+9+6+8 = 68 (RR)

Language = 12+1+14+7+21+1+7+5 = 68 (O)

Old Testament = 3+6+5+7+4+8+7+8+5+4+4+7 = 68 (RR) (Code comes from OT)

Planet = 16+12+1+14+5+20 = 68 (O)

Again, this entire code comes from the *Torah,* which is in tribute to the stars, and begins the Old Testament. And please keep in mind that planets to the ancients included the sun and moon, where the sun is the source of all existence. Because we're talking about creation, it absolutely fits into this discussion. There can be no life without it, thus there could be no creation. With no creation, there are no mathematics, language, or anything.

And with regards to the existence of this world, tracing back to the Greeks, and possibly further, are the geometric shapes known as the 5 Platonic Solids. The singular, 'Platonic Solid', not by chance, shares the Gematria of 68, and the word 'Platonic' alone, using Reverse Reduction, equates to 45, similar to how 'Geometry' equals 45 with Reduction; number 4 foundation, number 5 creation.

Platonic Solid = 7+3+1+2+6+5+9+3+10+6+3+9+4 = 68 (R, S10)

Platonic = 2+6+8+7+3+4+9+6 = 45 (RR)

Geometry = 7+5+6+4+5+2+9+7 = 45 (R)

Gematriot = 7+5+4+1+2+9+9+6+2 = 45 (R) (The plural of Gematria)

The 5 Platonic Solids are as follows:

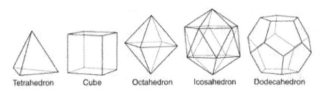

Tetrahedron   Cube   Octahedron   Icosahedron   Dodecahedron

The five 3-D shapes are the 4-sided Tetrahedron (representing fire), 6-sided Cube (earth), 8-sided Octahedron (air), 12-sided Icosahedron (water), and 20-sided Dodecahedron (energy / ether). In Plato's remembered work *Timaeus,* he theorized that all matter broke down to these geometric objects. His theory corresponded with the belief that God is the master mathematician, the Geometer of all existence, who brought all things into this world using mathematical intuition. For the record, the word 'Geometer' has Ordinal Gematria of 88, symbolizing the infinite, power, and strength, what is God, what is mathematics. While modern science has disproven that these shapes make up matter, Plato's theory was ultimately correct, that building blocks formed all existence, which we now refer to as atoms.

Out of these 5-geometric-shapes, that all share perfect symmetry, the one I want you to know about is the cube. The reason why is because it is the most relevant to this study, and an object we will discuss multiple times before the end cover. This object is extremely important to the Jewish faith, as well as Islam, and in the Jewish faith is commonly worn around the head during the time of prayer. In Judaism, it is known as 'Tefillin', having Reduction Gematria of 42, and Ordinal Gematria of 87, both numbers reducing to 6 in numerology terms, matching the sides of the cube, which are 6 in count. At the same time, the word 'Synagogue', where it is most commonly fastened to the forehead, also has Reduction Gematria of 42. As for the 6-dimensions of the object, if you add the numbers 1 through 6 together, they total 21, making 21 the 6th triangular number. This is fascinating because 'Saturn', the 6th planet from the sun, has Reduction Gematria of 21, same as *'Bible',* same as *'Jews'* when the letter S is counted for 10. Equally as interesting, if you write out 'twenty-one' as a word, it sums to '42' in the Reduction format, similar to 'Saturn', which equates to 42 in Reverse Reduction. Fittingly, it is the cube that is used to often symbolize Saturn. Also pertinent, the word 'cube' has Reduction Gematria of 13, what is the 6th prime number.

Tefillin = 2+5+6+9+3+3+9+5 = 42 (R)

Synagogue = 1+7+5+1+7+6+7+3+5 = 42 (R)

Twenty-one = 2+5+5+5+2+7 + 6+5+5 = 42 (R)

Bible = 2+9+2+3+5 = 21 (R); Jews = 1+5+5+10 = 21 (R, S10)

Cube = 3+3+2+5 = 13 (R)

Again, as we learned, the cube and the other Platonic Solids, are all born from Metatron's Cube, which is derived from the Flower of Life, the place we began the chapter. As you will recall, Metatron's Cube is composed of 13 circles, again, the 6th prime number, with the middle circle being encompassed by the cube. Please notice this fact about the object in the picture shown. Theoretically, the person who first created this object could have chosen to use more circles from the Flower of Life, but you now know why they did not. It is because of the prime number relationship with 13 and 6.

Also noteworthy, those who study in the footsteps of Plato are known as Platonists. The word 'Platonism' in Ordinal Gematria sums to 119, and the word 'Greece' in Reverse Ordinal also sums to 119. Metatron's Cube, containing each of the important Geometric objects to this fraternity of scholars also symbolizes the 'Star of David'. As we covered, and as a reminder, the words 'Orthodox' and 'Star of David' each equate to 119 in Ordinal Gematria, as does 'foundation'. To the Platonists, it is these five objects that make up the foundation for all things in existence.

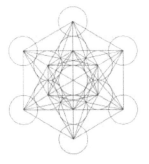

For our last piece on Sacred Geometry, I want to go back to where we began, the Flower of Life. Out of that shape also comes the Tree of Life, which is the physical representation for the spiritual belief system that is Kabbalah. In the chapter on Kabbalah, just ahead, we will learn what is so fascinating about this diagram. For now I just want you to appreciate that it is a component of Sacred Geometry, which is the bridge between letters and numbers, bringing much meaning to the study, and a necessary visual aid.

If you want to learn more about Sacred Geometry, I highly recommend the Disney Cartoon, 'Donald in Mathmagic Land', which pays homage to the Greeks. Appropriately, the title of the cartoon equates to 89, as does 'Donald Duck', 'Greek' and 'number', all in our four base ciphers, from Chapter 2, which I'll let you decipher and discover. If you want to take it a step further, using those same methods, unlock the numbers behind the word 'Pythagorean', and you'll quickly see why the cartoon was released in '59, on the date June 26. *In both Hebrew and in English, 'Freemasonry' sums to 59, but that's not all.

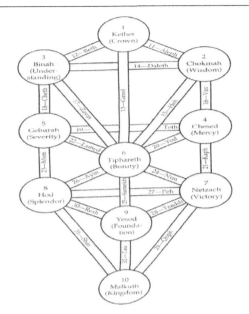

And for your learning pleasure, to the left is the Tree of Life, labeled, if you want to warm up for Chapter 8, where the focus is Kabbalah.

Do you notice how at the top of the diagram, the 'crown' connects one with 'God'? If you recall what you learned about those two words in Chapter 1, you'll be well on your way. Even better, if you take the Hebrew word, 'Kether', you should be able to calculate a Reduction value of 31, the 11th prime. As you learned, in Hebrew, Kabbalah has reduction Gematria of 11, the 'master' number, and only the master, can ever achieve the level of Kether. We'll get to it very soon truth seeker!

SEVEN

CHAPTER

━━━━━━━━━◄◯◯►━━━━━━━━━

Hermeticism, Alchemy & the 7 Classical Planets

Let us begin with definitions of Hermeticism and Alchemy courtesy of *Merriam-*

Webster's dictionary. The definitions are as follows:

Definition of Hermeticism:

1a: of or relating to the mystical and alchemical writings or teachings arising in the first three centuries C.E. and attributed to Hermes Trismegistus relating to or characterized by subjects that are mysterious and difficult to understand :relating to or characterized by occultism or abstruseness :recondite a hermetic discussion 2: from the belief that Hermes Trismegistus invented a magic seal to keep vessels airtight airtight hermetic seal impervious to external influence trapped inside the hermetic military machine —Jack Newfield recluse, solitary leads a hermetic life

Definition of Alchemy:

a medieval chemical science and speculative philosophy aiming to achieve the transmutation of the base metals into gold, the discovery of a universal cure for disease, and the discovery of a means of indefinitely prolonging life a power or process that changes or transforms something in a mysterious or impressive way ... the practitioners of financial alchemy that transformed the world of money in the 1980's ... —Gordon Williams an inexplicable or mysterious transmuting

As you can observe from the definitions, Hermeticism and Alchemy are related and having overlap, both being centered on the number 7. Ultimately, they're both regarding spiritual ascension and purification. Recall, the number 7 represents divine completion. In the definition for Hermeticism notice the use of the word 'seal'. This word having Gematria of 26, the number we first learned about in Chapter 1, is highly relevant. If you have ever read *Revelation*, there are 7-seals that are referenced in Chapters 5 through 8, that are components in the return of the Lord, the Son of God. In Ordinal Gematria, 'Seven Seals' equates to '*Revelation*', and in Reverse Ordinal Gematria, 'Seven Seals' also equates to '*Revelation*'. Please recall that in Reduction Gematria, *Revelation* equates to 49, what has a square root of 7. There can be no doubt that the 7-seals referenced in the concluding book of the *Bible* are in reference to the 7 Hermetic Principles, which also fall in line with the 7-sacred-chakras of the human body. Early Christians referred to the *prisca theologia*, meaning the one true religious doctrine, which is found in the teaching of Hermeticism, Zoroastrianism, Paganism, Hinduism and more. These same 7-principles are expressed in the most important text to Alchemy, which is known as '*The Kybalion*', having Reverse Reduction Gematria of '58', same as 'Seven Seals', not unlike the 7-seals being referenced in Chapters 5 through 8 of *Revelation*.

The Kybalion = 7+1+4 + 7+2+7+8+6+9+3+4 = 58 (RR)

Seven Seals = 10+5+4+5+5+10+5+1+3+10 = 58 (R, S10)

On a related note, the reported author of the 7 Hermetic Principles, originally found in the *Hermetic Corpus*, is Hermes Trismegistus, having Reduction Gematria of 85, the reflection of 58, and when 's' is counted for 10, having Gematria of 121, same as 'Revelation' and 'Seven Seals' in Ordinal. As you know, the number 121 has a square root of 11, and when you sum 1 through 11, it totals 66, much like *Revelation* being the 66th book of the Bible. As we learned in Chapter 5, the 11 is the master number, and these are master teachings, from the one said to be most masterful of all by the Greeks.

Hermes Trismegistus = 8+5+9+4+5+1+2+9+9+1+4+5+7+9+1+2+3+1 = 85 (R)

Hermes   Trismegistus   = 8+5+9+4+5+10+2+9+9+10+4+5+7+9+10+2+3+10 = 121 (R, S10)

Even more, as mentioned, these teachings are considered to be part of the 'prisca theologia', what all the world's religions are centered on. This term, shares a Reverse Reduction value of 85, as well as 121 when 'p' is recognized as 11, and 'h' as 10.

Prisca Theologia = 2+9+9+8+6+8+7+1+4+3+6+3+2+9+8 = 85 (RR)

Prisca Theologia = 11+9+9+8+6+8+7+10+22+3+6+3+2+9+8 = 121 (RR, P11, H10)

Better than that, the title *Hermetic Corpus* sums to 74 in Reduction Gematria, matching the Ordinal value of 'Masonic' and so much more. Let us not forget that number 7 is the 4th prime number, and the divisors of the number 4, sum to 7. When we arrive at our chapter on Christianity, the greater significance of this number, 74, what is the reflection of 47, will be unlocked. For the time being, recall that Revelation is about the return of 'Jesus', summing to 74 using the Ordinal method (74 is 11 in numerology terms).

Hermetic Corpus = 8+5+9+4+5+2+9+3+3+6+9+7+3+1 = 74 (R)

Jesus = 10+5+19+21+19 = 74 (O)

And on the same train of thought, the overlap with Christianity and the Hermetic Corpus, let us examine the 'Gematriot' overlap of 'Hermetic' and 'Holy Bible'. Keep in mind 'Gematriot' and 'Gematria' each have Gematria of 45.

Hermetic = 8+5+9+4+5+2+9+3 = 45 (R)

Hermetic = 1+4+9+5+4+7+9+6 = 45 (RR)

Holy Bible = 8+6+3+7+2+9+2+3+5 = 45 (R)

Holy Bible = 1+3+6+2+7+9+7+6+4 = 45 (RR)

Do not discount that both titles begin with H, the 8th letter. As we learned, this numerical digit represents the infinite, balance, symmetry, power, and strength. In light of this symbolism, let us now examine the 7-principles, which encompass these values.

1. Mentalism – "THE ALL IS MIND; The Universe is Mental."
2. Correspondence – "As above, so below; as below, so above."
3. Vibration – "Nothing rests; everything moves; everything vibrates."
4. Polarity – "Everything is Dual; everything has poles; everything has its pair of opposites; like and unlike are the same; opposites are identical in nature, but different in degree; extremes meet; all truths are but half-truths; all paradoxes may be reconciled."
5. Rhythm – "Everything flows, out and in; everything has its tides; all things rise and fall; the pendulum-swing manifests in everything; the measure of the swing to the right is the measure of the swing to the left; rhythm compensates."
6. Cause and Effect – "Every cause has its Effect; every Effect has its Cause; everything happens according to Law; Chance is but a name for Law not recognized; there are many planes of causation, but nothing escapes the Law."
7. Gender – Gender is in everything; everything has its Masculine and Feminine Principles; Gender manifests on all planes."

Let's put into terms what these 7-principles mean and how they relate to the overall study of this book, the significance of language, letters and numbers and the spiritual significance behind their relationship. Again, the purpose of Kabbalah is to understand God, so that we mortal souls can grow to be more like 'The Creator', increasing our understanding of our existence, as well as our appreciation for being here, and our happiness with it. Mentalism is much the same, recognizing that the mind holds the power to improve our state of being, no matter how bad or good our surroundings are at any particular moment. All is mind, and all can be achieved with the mind. The next principle, Correspondence, is intuitive. What happens above happens below. Simply put, we are 'stardust', and what takes place within the stars, takes place within us. If you have ever studied astrology, you are likely aware of how your date of birth impacts the person you are, from the way you behave, to the way you think, to what your innermost ambitions are. The third principle, Vibration, is a big one. In fact, it is what gives meaning to this entire study. Everything carries a vibration, including every number, and these vibrations impact our state of consciousness and our behavior. Much like astrology, if you have ever read about personal numerology, corresponding with your date of birth, and your personal name Gematria, you have learned that the numbers associated with you, which are the digits 1 through 9 and the master numbers 11 and 22, dictate what you are as an individual. What often sounds like hocus pocus to common-folk becomes gospel when this knowledge is studied and applied. For you the reader, I personally recommend decoding your own name; your parents' names; your friends' names; your children's names; and your other loved ones' names; as well as the date of births for each. What you will find will be seemingly magical when you compare the numbers of those around you, with your own, mark my words, it never fails. In the final chapter, I will share with you my own characteristics to help inspire. What is true for me is true for all of us. The fourth principle, Polarity, speaks to the dualism of this world. If you have ever done something kind for

73

someone, and something horrible happened to you in return, this is exactly what this principle speaks to. Essentially it is communicating the world is in balance, and this is how balance works. You do something good, and bam! Just like that, something bad comes right back at you. If you've ever noticed how tyrants get away with murder, that's the other side of the coin. I don't know about you truth seeker, but the most dishonest people I know, also seem to have the best luck. But please, don't let that be a reason to turn to the dark side. Instead, realize, to maintain the balance, the world needs those who have pure souls, which I imagine you are, as someone who sought out this book, the truth seeker. As for number five, Rhythm, I think you probably already understand. What goes around comes around. The sixth principle, Cause and Effect, reminds that there are no coincidences. Every action determines an equal and opposite reaction. Think of it like this, we as people, are dominos, and what we do in the world, in terms of every action, leads to some sort of output. This is why it is important to be good in nature, because if more people were, we could see a greater positive effect in the chain of humanity. And the concluding principle, the seventh, Gender, speaks for itself. If you were not aware, numbers are even assigned a masculine and feminine, thanks to Pythagoras and the Greeks, and possibly those who came before them. According to Pythagoras, odd numbers were masculine, and even numbers were feminine. This is largely because of the number 3, which symbolizes strength and power, not to say that women aren't strong and powerful, but in terms of physical prowess, men are more gifted in this regard, at least typically.

If you want to boil down the 7-principles further, they amount to the Golden Rule, which is the heart of all spiritual teachings. The Golden Rule is, "do unto others as you would have done unto you." If you have never taken the time to consider the essence of this simple teaching, it is based in the concept that when you do right, you make the world a better place, and you help the next person in line do right as well. Of course the 7-principles are more detailed and specific, but they are trying to communicate to the reader the significance of understanding the consequences of our actions and how positivity and positive actions can improve our state of being and create more positive outcomes in the world we all share, even in the face of adversity, as we so often battle with. It's mathematics. Just for a moment, imagine a world where everyone operated by the Golden Rule. Imagine. It could be glorious. It all begins with the mental. Let us now compare 'Golden Rule' with 'Hermes Trismegistus', the author of the 7-principles.

Golden Rule = 7+15+12+4+5+14 + 18+21+12+5 = 113 (O)

Hermes Trismegistus =
1+4+9+5+4+8+7+9+9+8+5+4+2+9+8+7+6+8 = 113 (RR)

Golden Rule = 2+3+6+5+22+4 + 9+6+6+22 = 85 (RR, E22)

Hermes Trismegistus =
8+5+9+4+5+1+2+9+9+1+4+5+7+9+1+2+3+1 = 85 (R)

Also relevant, 'Golden Rule' has Reverse Reduction Gematria of 49, like the Reduction Gematria of *Revelation*, which has a square root of 7, brining us back to the 7-principles.

Golden Rule = 2+3+6+5+4+4 + 9+6+6+4 = 49 (RR)

For good measure, let's compare in Gematria terms, the words 'revelation', 'epiphany' and 'apocalypse', with the latter word, in Greek, meaning "uncovering", or "having a breakthrough", not unlike the words revelation and epiphany.

Revelation = 9+5+4+5+3+1+2+9+6+5 = 49 (R)

Epiphany = 5+7+9+7+8+1+5+7 = 49 (R)

Apocalypse = 8+2+3+6+8+6+2+2+8+4 = 49 (RR)

In the *Bible,* in *Daniel 12:4,* it states that the "seals" are not to be understood until the end of the Age, which is certainly the age of Pisces, which we are now living; and appropriately, these same 7-seals are a major component to the conclusion of the *Holy Bible* where they are presented with much mystery and intrigue, not unlike the words surrounding *Revelation 13:18* about the number of the beast. Well here we are truth seeker, reaching the end of the age, and the time is now for us as people to overcome, and to have the great awakening many of us have been longing for. We must change our course and we must heal our transgressions, now and not later. Here we have the knowledge to comprehend, understand and act upon, and all the reasons to do so. The verse from *Daniel*, prophesizing what is to come, is as follows.

Daniel 12:4 New International Version (NIV) "But you, Daniel, roll up and seal the words of the scroll until the time of the end. Many will go here and there to increase knowledge."

We are most certainly increasing knowledge. Appropriately, the *Book of Daniel* is a biblical apocalypse, combining the prophecy of history with the study of the end of days, which is both cosmic in its teachings and political in its nature. It is very much a precursor to Revelation, which despite concluding the *New Testament,* is entirely based in the *Old Testament.* Also intriguing, is that *Daniel* is the 27th book of the *Old Testament,* and using Reduction Gematria, *'Daniel'* sums to 27.

Moving on, as stated in the definition we began with, Alchemy is important knowledge to the occult, including Freemasonry. Once again, the word occult means hidden, it does not mean evil or have any nefarious connotations with it, even though it is often considered in such light. Despite the fact that some factions of Freemasonry and other secret societies are operating for nefarious purposes, this is not their true intent. The true intent is known as the 'mystical ascent', having Reduction Gematria of 47, like the degrees on the Freemason logo, as we learned. The mystical ascent is a fancy way of saying connecting with God by unlocking the hidden knowledge that brings one closer to their maker, including that of Hermeticism and Alchemy. Appropriately, the names 'Hermeticism', 'Alchemy' and 'Freemasonry' have overlap in Gematria. As we decode, keep in mind the number 6 represents perfection, and the number 7 connects to divine completion. Again, Hermeticism, Alchemy and Freemasonry are involved efforts in the pursuit of spiritual perfection, completing what lacks within, and attaining the divine; at least this is what they are intended to be.

Hermeticism = 1+4+9+5+4+7+9+6+9+8+5 = 67 (RR)

Alchemy = 1+12+3+8+5+13+25 = 67 (O)

Freemasonry = 6+9+5+5+4+1+10+6+5+9+7 = 67 (R, S10)

On a related note, '*Revelation*', in Reduction, when 'v' is accounted for as 22, also sums to 67, as does '*The Kybalion*' when 'h' is accounted for as 10. As a reminder, if you read *Revelation*, it is full of 7, and of course, teaches of 666 (6 and 7).

Revelation = 9+5+22+5+3+1+2+9+6+5 = 67 (R, V22)

The Kybalion = 7+10+4+7+2+7+8+6+9+3+4 = 67 (RR, H10)

As we learned to start the chapter, the 7-seals of *Revelation* are truly the 7 Hermetic Principles, as described in *The Kybalion* and the *Hermetic Corpus,* important to both Hermeticism and Alchemy. Both Hermeticism and Alchemy originate from Egypt, the civilization that was born from the Babylonians and which gave rise to the Greeks, where Pythagoras and Plato learned the wisdom they taught to their followers, including that of Gematria and Isopsephy. As we have covered, it was the Greeks who wrote *Revelation* and it is the same Greeks who are credited with creating the *Hermetic Corpus,* where the 7-principles originate according to modern historians. That said, it is often stated all roads lead to Rome, but if you keep traveling, the same road goes through Greece, Egypt, Babylon, the Far East and possibly further. Since we live in an age where history has been buried, destroyed, distorted and purposefully recreated, we must recognize that much has been lost, some never to be recovered. I make this point so that you remember when I say something is credited to someone, it is entirely possible that despite the credit being placed where it is in modern times, it might not be entirely true.

Back on the subject of the 'mystical ascent', in modern practice, Alchemy is primarily focused on transmuting states of consciousness to achieve higher spiritual planes, more so that transmuting lead into gold. As we stated earlier, this is not unlike Kabbalah, which is also pertaining to spiritual ascension and enlightenment. For a little more Gematria, I want to decode the word 'transmute' using both Reduction and Reverse Reduction methods to shed more light on the overlap between Freemasonry, Hermeticism, Alchemy and Kabbalah.

Transmute = 2+9+1+5+1+4+3+2+5 = 32 (R)

Transmute = 7+9+8+4+8+5+6+7+4 = 58 (RR)

Take note of the output of number 32, the Masonic degree coming just before the sacred 33rd-degree, and don't forget the relationship with the number 58 and Freemasonry as well as *The Kybalion*, or that the 7-seals are written about in Chapters 5 through 8 of *Revelation*. In Kabbalah, on the Tree of Life, there are 32 spiritual paths, which you can examine from the conclusion of the last chapter. *The Book of Formation,* the foundational text of Kabbalah, begins with its first sentence, *"In thirty-two mysterious paths of wisdom did the Lord write, the Lord of Hosts, the God of Israel, the Living Elohim, and King of the Universe, the Almighty, Merciful, and Gracious God; He is great and exalted and eternally dwelling in the Height, His name is holy, He is exalted and holy."* The very next sentence is where we began the first chapter. *"He created His Universe by the three forms of expression: Numbers, Letters, and Words."*

Knowing that Kabbalah, Hermeticism and Alchemy are foundational pieces of the teachings within Masonic Lodges, I want to revisit the quote from Albert Pike, from his opus, *Morals and Dogma.* Within he writes, *"One is filled with admiration, on penetrating into the Sanctuary of the Kabbalah, at seeing a doctrine so logical, so simple, and at the same time so absolute. The necessary union of ideas and signs, the consecration of the most fundamental realities by the primitive characters; the Trinity of Words, Letters, and Numbers; a philosophy simple as the alphabet, profound and infinite as the Word; theorems more complete and luminous than those of Pythagoras; a theology summed up by counting on one's fingers; an Infinite which can be held in the hollow of an infant's hand; ten ciphers and twenty-two letters, a triangle, a square, and a circle, these are all the elements of the Kabbalah. These are the elementary principles of the written Word, reflection of that spoken Word that created the world!"*

Pay mind to the fact that he uses the word 'sanctuary' in reference to what is contained within Kabbalah. It is no coincidence he chose this specific word, in light of the 32-paths of Kabbalah, from *The Book of Formation.* As we learned, every number carries a vibration, which means every word does just the same. Let us now decode the word 'Sanctuary' using the Reduction and Reverse Reduction methods to find a familiar pattern in numbers, again, 32 and 58.

Sanctuary = 1+1+5+3+2+3+1+9+7 = 32 (R)

Sanctuary = 8+8+4+6+7+6+8+9+2 = 58 (RR)

In Chapter 2, we learned the significance of 32, 58 and 187 in relation to Freemasonry, the establishment of the United States, and its capital, Washington D.C., where the statute of Pike with *Morals and Dogma* is immortalized. On the subject, let us decode the word 'transmutation'; the word describing what Alchemy is all about, transmuting oneself from the place they currently are, to a better place, a more spiritually enlightened place, more in tune with oneself, their surroundings and God. To do so, we will use the most relevant of the Kabbalah ciphers, ALW Kabbalah, to uncover one more 187.

Transmutation = 24+12+1+14+5+21+17+24+1+24+23+7+14 = 187 (ALW Kabbalah)

Please recall that there are 187-chapters in the *Torah*, the source code for the relationship between letters and numbers, and the word 'Elohim', in Hebrew, equates to 187. Again, in Alchemy, you are using the Hermetic philosophy to transmute your state of being, to raise your spiritual vibration, and to connect with 'The Creator', or expressed otherwise, 'Elohim'. As a second related reminder, it is the belief of Kabbalists, that by understanding the numerical code behind the letters of language, you can better interpret the spiritual texts, from the *Hebrew Bible* to the *Holy Bible*, as well as the events and signs around you, helping achieve the same desired outcome of spiritual ascension. It is the totality of the knowledge that the occultists seek to make the path most attainable.

Also, on the subject of transmutation, let us cover the 7-Classical Planets, also known as the 7-Luminaries, and the 7-metals that are associated with each of the celestial bodies. To the Greeks, the word planet meant "wanderer", and they earned this name because they were the only objects in the sky wandering to the naked eye. It is for these 7-heavenly bodies that we have the 7-days of the week, as we learned about in Chapter 5. In Alchemy, the sun is associated with gold, the moon with silver, Mars with iron, Mercury with quicksilver (what we commonly call mercury), Jupiter with tin, Venus with copper, and Saturn with lead. Above all, notice it is the sun representing gold, and Saturn representing Lead. The moon representing silver is also fascinating and later you will learn about *The Wizard of Oz* and why Dorothy wore silver slippers on the yellow brick (gold) road in the book version of the story, which is entirely related. Dorothy and Toto aside, most commonly in Alchemy you will hear the reference of Lead into Gold, meaning from one end of the spectrum to the opposite, playing on the principle of Polarity. As we mentioned earlier, it is the sun that is 93-million-miles from earth, the true keeper of time, and it is 'Saturn', the most distant of the planets to the ancients and having Ordinal Gematria of 93 that is considered to be the keeper of time by the occult. Understand, it is no coincidence that these two heavenly objects, the bookends of time of the 7-Luminaries, represent Gold and Lead in this ancient study, and share overlap in letters and numbers.

80

Instead, it is a reminder of duality, and how everything in this world has an equal and an opposite. As we covered, Hermeticism originates from Egypt and Greece, and it is Egypt where the legend of Horus, the son of Osiris and Isis, who represents the sun and the moon, comes from. In that same legend, as briefly discussed in Chapter 5, it is where Horus avenges his father's murderer, Set, who is the planet Saturn, again bringing the two heavenly objects together (in the chapter on murder by numbers, you'll discover the significance of number 44, representing 'kill' in Ordinal, same as how 'Set' sums to 44, not unlike 'clock').

While we're on the subject, I should mention that a famous story from 1993, that of Lorena Bobbitt cutting off her husband's penis, John Wayne Bobbitt's, and throwing it out the window, never for it to be found again, was a complete hoax, and a major tribute to the story of Osiris's lost penis, which was also never recovered. It is said that John Bobbitt's birthday was March 23, 1967, emphasis on '67, for 'Hermeticism', 'Alchemy' and 'Freemasonry'; and the date his penis was reportedly cut off was June 23, 1993, emphasis on '93, which was his 93rd day of being 26-years old. Recall that 'Sun God' has Reduction Gematria of 26, along with a host of other Gods relating to the sun, most notably Apollo. If you look further, his birth numerology also equates to 93, as follows.

*3/23/67 = 3+23+67 = 93

Adding to the riddle is the Reduction Gematria of the name Lorena Bobbitt, which equates to 54, just the same as 'sun', 'Horus', 'Osiris', and 'love', where in their case, intercourse would no longer be a part of the equation, at least according to media reports.

Lorena Bobbitt = 3+6+9+5+5+1+2+6+2+2+9+2+2 = 54 (R)

Sun = 19+21+14 = 54 (O); Horus = 19+12+9+6+8 = 54 (RO)

Osiris = 10+15+0+14+0+15 = 54 (LCH Kabbalah)

*Love = 12+15+22+5 = 54 (O); *Love = 15+12+5+22 = 54 (RO)

Lorena Bobbitt equates to 187 as well, a number connecting to Elohim and the Torah as we have covered, as well as the phrase 'Unconquered Sun', which originates out of Rome, and was the title given to the light in the sky by those who worshipped the sun, including many early Christians, who perceived the sun as God's love, and a spiritual force. Unconquered Sun as well as Sol Invictus were two names predating Jesus.

Lorena Bobbitt = 38+15+18+5+14+1+28+15+2+2+9+20+20 = 187 (Francis Bacon)

Unconquered Sun = 6+13+24+12+13+10+6+22+9+22+23+8+6+13 = 187 (RO)

On the subject of early Christianity, notice the overlap in Gematria with 'Christianity' and 'Unconquered Sun', while thinking about the words 'son' and 'sun', in terms of the common phrase used in modern Christianity by English speaking people, the "Son of God", or "God's Son", titles we'll learn more about in the chapters ahead, but which you are more than welcome to decode now to get ahead of the curve.

Christianity = 3+8+9+9+1+2+9+1+5+9+2+7 = 65 (R)

Unconquered Sun = 3+5+3+6+5+8+3+5+9+5+4+1+3+5 = 65 (R)

For a historical note, it was the Council of Nicea of 325 CE where the Sun God, known as Sol Invictus, or the Unconquered Sun, became also known as Jesus. In light of Freemasonry being a major part of our understanding of Christianity as we do through the English translations of the Bibles, let us examine the Ordinal Gematria of 'Scottish Rite of Freemasonry', which equates to 325, and most definitely not by coincidence.

Scottish Rite of Freemasonry = 19+3+15+20+20+9+19+8+18+9+20+5+15+6+6+18+5+5+13+1+19+15+14+18+25 = 325 (O)

82

To close out our parallel to the story of the Bobbitt's, the surname 'Bobbitt' has Reverse Reduction Gematria of 47, the number representing 'time', as well as 'authority', where time is the ultimate authority. The number 47 also syncs with the degrees of separation for the Tropics of Cancer and Capricorn as we have learned. Even better, 'Bobbitt' has Reverse Ordinal Gematria of 119, the number corresponding with 'all seeing eye', where the sun is the true symbolism of this well known title. And let us not forget, the purpose of these stories is to capture the mind's eye of the masses, which the Bobbitt story no doubt did for millions. I was just a boy when it was breaking news, but it's a story I'll personally never forget, and even knowing what a hoax it is, I'm feeling sore in my shorts right now just thinking about it, just as I felt sore in my shorts the first time I heard the news. The media tyrants, who contrive the propaganda, they're very much aiming to impact our mental state, and always in a negative way. Again, the mental is the key, in Hermeticism and in Alchemy, which Freemasonry has roots in, and which the tyrants are well studied.

Bobbitt = 7+3+7+7+9+7+7 = 47 (RR)

Bobbitt = 25+12+25+25+18+7+7 = 119 (RO)

It's also worth mentioning that the name 'Bobbitt' connects to 'sun' and 'Horus' through the Septenary method as follows.

Bobbitt = 2+2+2+2+5+7+7 = 27 (Septenary)

Sun = 8+6+13 = 27 (RO)

Horus = 8+6+9+3+1 = 27 (R)

Horus = 1+3+9+6+8 = 27 (RR)

Moving on, to draw another parallel between the sun and Saturn, from earth we have our clearest view of Saturn every 54-weeks and as we have learned, in Gematria terms, 'sun' sums to 54 in Ordinal, while 'Horus' sums to 54 in Reverse Ordinal, clearly illustrating the significant relationship between these two Classical Planets that have been studied for eons to chart the course of time. Tying in with the coding of the number 54, in both Ordinal, and Reverse Ordinal, 'eyes' equates to 54, having perfect symmetry, just as they do on our respective faces. If it weren't for our eyes, we wouldn't be able to appreciate these amazing and mathematically inclined relationships in the sky. Even more, the legend is that Horus's right eye became the sun, and his left eye became the moon, after winning his battle with his nemesis Set, avenging his father. Through these stories and legends, we can clearly see how the stars above have been used throughout time to create the belief systems we abide by below on earth; again, *as above, so below.* And you should know by now, these beliefs aren't arbitrary, instead, they are the products of countless years of observation, mapping, ingenuity, and mankind coming to understand that what is taking place above, is ruling over what's below, knowledge that has largely been forgotten in modern times.

To illustrate this point, in the *Bible,* there are 189-mentions of Gold. Again, the sun represents Gold in Hermeticism and Alchemy, and the sun is also the true representation of Jesus Christ, what is God's love for all of humanity, unconditional, who died for our sins, and who returned to life, before ascending into the Heavens. Knowing that there are 189-mentions of Gold in the *Bible,* please admire the Gematria of the word 'reincarnate', where every single day, the 'sun' dies at night, and reincarnates in the morning.

Reincarnate = 9+22+18+13+24+26+9+13+26+7+22 = 189 (RO)

Resurrection = 12+25+5+17+12+12+25+13+24+23+7+14 = 189 (ALK Kabbalah)

Reincarnate = 9+5+9+5+3+1+9+5+1+2+5 = 54 (R)

Even better, 'reincarnate' also shares Gematria of 108, reminding that the sun is said to have a diameter that is 108-earths across, and be the distance of 108-suns from the earth. Please also recall how this number connects to 'Geometry', and how the *Bible* also shares Gematria corresponding with Geometry. As a reminder, it is God who is the master mathematician, and who according to Kabbalists, has built this world with letters, number and language.

Reincarnate = 9+22+9+4+6+8+9+4+8+7+22 = 108 (O)

To close this chapter I want to make an important point. *The Kybalion,* published in 1908, the Hermetic and Alchemical text, where the 7-principles are recorded for achieving spiritual mastery, has credited authors known as *The Three Initiates,* who claim to be the spirit of Hermes Trismegistus. Hermes Trismegistus throughout history has been said to be a mortal man, a living God, a God above, and a complete fiction. Depending on whom you talk to, the same can be said about the likes of Jesus Christ, and other spiritual figures. In the case of Hermes, as we learned, he is the centerpiece of the closely related spiritual system known as Hermeticism and the supposed author of the *Hermetic Corpus,* which has many parallels to Christianity, as covered. What all historians concur on regarding Hermes is that he is a character from Greek culture, and is the reincarnation of Thoth, the Egyptian God of reading, writing, language, mathematics, thought and more, whose existence is also debated. There are many who contend Thoth was made up so that the Egyptians could take credit for the advancements of the Babylonians who came before them. According to Manly P. Hall, Thoth is the author of 26,000 books, quite an accomplishment! And as you will recall from Chapter 1, in Reduction Gematria, Thoth sums to 26, same as God in Ordinal, and same as Babylon. And it is just that which brings me to the concluding point. When it comes to God, I think we are wise to respect the beliefs of all, from Hermes, to Thoth, to Horus, to Jesus, and more, so long as one's beliefs are not harmful to others. Ultimately, all faiths have parallels, and no one is all right or all wrong. To claim that your beliefs are superior to anyone else's is to be ignorant of history and what our ancestors have taught us. In Hermeticism, there is no absolute truth in the same way there is no such thing as absolute cold, or absolute hot. If you have ever come from a frigid environment, the touch of mildly warm water may feel comforting, but that same water temperature on a hot summer's day, might feel equally as cool and refreshing, or possibly even too warm due to the already hot temperature surrounding. Thus, all truths are based in perspective, and as the mortal souls we are, we can never have enough perspective to entertain what is fully true, or untrue. These are words to the wise. For a few more words, please be open to knowledge, and take what is given, and use what is worthy. I know that in the *Bible* and other spiritual texts it tells the reader to take the words within the book as the absolute authority while ignoring the words of others, and these same texts are credited to being the words of God and if not obeyed there might be consequences, but please use reason. As I have taught my students, God is not in the business of writing books, but God is in all of us, and God has given us discernment to detect right and wrong, and truth from lies, however challenging it may be sometimes. And of course, please use that same advice with every word written in this book. As the author, my only intention is to shed knowledge on what has been hidden from the masses for far too long, and what in my opinion is deserved to be known by all. Going forward let the light shine and let the Golden Rule guide you.

*And before totally saying goodbye to this chapter, I'll give you a few more Gematria notes to consider. Keep in mind the sun in the sky is adorned by the 12-constellations, not unlike Jesus and his 12-disciples, making 13, what is the 7th Fibonacci number, which are said to be the numbers God used to create the world we share, that we will learn more about in the chapters ahead.

Son of God = 1+6+5+6+6+7+6+4 = 41 (R)

Christ = 3+8+9+9+10+2 = 41 (R)

King = 11+9+14+7 = 41 (O)

Crucify = 6+9+6+6+9+3+2 = 41 (RR)

41, the 13th prime number; *JC = 10+3 = 13

86

Lock = 12+15+3+11 = 41 (O); Key = 11+5+25 = 41 (O); Open = 3+2+4+4 = 13 (RR)

In light of the 7-seals; Christ = 77 (O); Seventy-Seven = 49 (R); Revelation = 49 (R)

Seventy-Seven = 149 (RO); Revelation = 149 (RO); Seven Seals = 149 (RO)

EIGHT

CHAPTER

◄─❮◯◯❯─►

Kabbalah and the Tree of Life, Roots of the Code

To the left is what is known as the Tree of Life, the visual model for the mysticism known as Kabbalah. It is the representation of the path of spiritual ascension, mimicking the structure of the human body, from the head (Kether) to the genitals (Yesod), which includes 32-paths as we have briefly become familiar with in earlier chapters. Even more, the Tree of life is also considered to be a map of the universe and the psyche, as well as the order of the creation of the cosmos; *as above, so below*. Recall, this Tree is derived

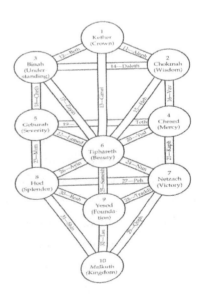

from the Flower of Life, composed of 61-circles, which we learned of in the chapter on Sacred Geometry. You will notice in the diagram for the Tree of Life, there are 22-paths and 10-circles. Let us not forget about the 'Master Builder' number, 22. The circles are known collectively as Sephirot (or Sefirot), and individually as Sephirah (or Sefirah). Before we begin to examine what is significant about the Tree of Life and its respective components, I want you to know that there are various spellings used for the name Kabbalah, where Kabbalah is the most traditional spelling and what is used within the Jewish faith. When the Tree of Life is used outside of the Jewish faith by the occult, it is spelled Qabalah. Thus when Kabbalah is practiced within Freemasonry, it is Qabalah, and not Kabbalah, and when it is practiced with Christianity, it is Cabbala and not Kabbalah either. Other spellings you might encounter are as follows: Kabbala, Kaballah, Kabala, Kabballah, Kabalah, Kaballa, Kabballa, Cabbalah, Cabbala, Caballah, Cabala, Cabballah, Cabalah, Caballa, Cabballa, Qabbalah, Qabbala, Qaballah, Qabala, Qabballah, Qabalah, Qaballa, and Qabballa. For the purpose of this book, we will just entertain the spellings of Kabbalah, Qabalah and Cabbala, as they are most common.

With the many and counting spellings of the name out of the way, I want to decode the most appropriate, 'Kabbalah', as well as the name 'Tree of Life', and its Hebrew name, 'Etz haChayim', as well as 'Gematria' and 'Sephirot'. You will notice that each word has a Gematria value of '52' in Reverse Reduction. Recall that in Chapter 2 we learned 'Authority', among other related words shares this numerical value of 52, and traditionally, Kabbalah was knowledge for elites, *the cabal,* and people in positions of authority, which is exactly what it would still be today without the release of this book, or the teachings I have been spreading online since 2013, as well as those who have learned from me and now teach the knowledge as well, from blogs to YouTube videos. Consider that means this knowledge had been a secret from the masses since the Renaissance, and really longer, which means this revealing couldn't be any more overdue. Also significant, in Francis Bacon Gematria, 'God' sums to 52, and one more time, this Tree is for connecting with the Most High, and is used by people across many faiths.

Authority = 8+6+7+1+3+9+9+7+2 = 52 (RR)

*The Cabal = 20+8+5+3+1+2+1+12 = 52 (O)

Kabbalah = 7+8+7+7+8+6+8+1 = 52 (RR)

Gematria = 2+4+5+8+7+9+9+8 = 52 (RR)

Tree of Life = 7+9+4+4 + 3+3 + 6+9+3+4 = 52 (RR)

Etz haChayim = 4+7+1+1+8+6+1+8+2+9+5 = 52 (RR)

Sephirot = 8+4+2+10+9+9+3+7 = 52 (RR, H10); God = 33+15+4 = 52 (Francis Bacon)

Ultimately, the purpose of the Tree of Life is to model the path to spiritual enlightenment, where when the student reaches the crown, a near impossible task to achieve, they are united with God. The terminology often used to describe this purpose is 'divine emanation' having Reduction Gematria of 74, and Reverse Reduction Gematria of 88. Keep in mind 'Jewish' sums to 74 in Ordinal, and 88 in Reverse Ordinal. Recall how Jews commonly spell the name of God as G-d, or what is 7-4. Also pertinent, the word 'emanation' alone has Reverse Reduction Gematria of '52', and Reduction Gematria of '38', the latter of which matches the Ordinal value of Kabbalah as covered in Chapter 2.

Emanation = 4+5+8+4+8+7+9+3+4 = 52 (RR)

On the subject, 'crown' shares Gematria of 26, same as 'God', and 'Tree of Life' has Ordinal Gematria of 101, what is the 26th prime, as we learned about in the opening chapter. For good measure, let's do the math. As you likely know, hard work is the only way to the top, from Kabbalah, to everything else in this world.

Tree of Life = 20+18+5+5+15+6+12+9+6+5 = 101 (O)

God = 7+15+4 = 26 (O); Crown = 6+9+3+4+4 = 26 (RR)

Not by chance, both 'Tree of Life' and 'Etz haChayim' also share Gematria corresponding with the word 'light'. In the words of Manly P. Hall, Freemasonry is about the pursuit of light, and again, both he and Albert Pike acknowledge that the Masonic brotherhood is very much rooted in Kabbalah, among other esoteric belief systems, such as that of the Kundalini.

Tree of Life = 2+9+5+5+6+6+3+9+6+5 = 56 (R)

Etz haChayim = 5+2+8 + 8+1+3+8+1+7+9+4 = 56 (R)

Light = 12+9+7+8+20 = 56 (O)

*Three = 20+8+18+5+5 = 56 (O)

Do not overlook that the number 56 breaks down to 11, the master number. As we covered in Chapter 2, 'Kabbalah' sums to 38 in English Ordinal and Hebrew Ordinal, also breaking down to number 11. As you should recall, in Hebrew Reduction, Kabbalah sums to 11 as well. This is appropriate because as we learned in Chapter 5, the number 11 symbolizes the all powerful, and again, the Tree of Life's purpose is for the person using its wisdom to connect with The Creator. At the same time, the number 52 that we just decoded from the title of the Tree of Life breaks down to number 7, symbolizing divine completion. For the Kabbalist who ascends to the top of the tree, they will have completed the divine mission.

As you look at the Tree of Life, please notice there are three main pillars. They are the Pillar of Mercy on the right, the Pillar of Severity on the left, and the Pillar of Balance in the center. As we learned in Chapter 5, the words 'three' and 'light' have much in common in Gematria, and it is the third verse of Genesis where God brings light into the world. The Pillar of Mercy is found on the right hand side of the Tree, and is associated with the left side of the human body, as well as the right-brain. It is composed of the following Sephirot- Chokmah, Chesed and Netzach. The top sphere on the right pillar is Chokmah and is the sphere of Yang, the highest sphere of the masculine, whereas the spheres below it are considered to be feminine. Don't forget our 7 Hermetic Principles, where the seventh is Gender. For a parallel you're likely familiar with, the top Sefirah that is Yang is also displayed in the famous Taoist symbol, Yin & Yang. Chokmah represents wisdom, Chesed represents grace and Netzach represents persistence.

Complimenting the Pillar of Mercy, the Pillar of Severity stands on the left hand side of the Tree of life, but it represents the right side of the human body. Of course, it is associated with left-brain functions, opposite of the Pillar of Mercy. It is composed of the following Sephirot- Binah, Geburah, and Hod. Binah is said to be the Great Sea and is the sphere of Yin, the highest aspects of the feminine principles, whereas the lower spheres, representing war and science respectively, are generally considered to be masculine. Naturally, this is the Yin, opposite Yang, from the same Taoist symbol. As was mentioned in Chapter 6, all spiritualties and religions draw their significance from Sacred Geometry and the circle, thus why there are parallels between Kabbalah and Taoism, as well as so much more. Binah symbolizes repentance and reason, where Geburah is judgment and determination and Hod steadfastness and sincerity.

Next up is what rests in the middle of the Tree of Life; it is the Pillar of Balance. Rightfully so, being in the middle, it is associated with balance, holism and integration. The word holism pertains to the entirety, distinguishing the fact that the parts of a system cannot be separated or they are rendered useless. To make the point clear, think about the body without the brain, or the heart, or the lungs. We humans are very machine-like, and all components of our body are working in unison. Granted, some parts of the body can be lost, such as limbs, but what is in the center of us, the vital organs, they are irreplaceable, and this is what is symbolized in the Pillar of Balance. Again, as mentioned, the Tree of Life ultimately is a physical representation of our own human anatomy, something we learned many secrets about to begin this journey in Chapter 1. The Pillar of Balance is composed of the following spheres- Kether, Tipareth, Yesod and Malkuth. Starting with Kether, it is the crown, symbolizing what is not to be understood,

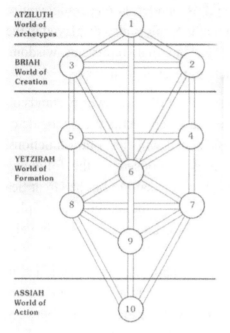

ATZILUTH
World of
Archetypes

BRIAH
World of
Creation

YETZIRAH
World of
Formation

ASSIAH
World of
Action

because it is God, and man is not capable of comprehending the ways of God. It is commonly referred to as the Zohar, what is also the title of the sacred text to Kabbalah. Many Kabbalists will simply state the Kether represents the unknown, and what is to remain unknown. Below the Kether is the Tipareth, symbolizing the Heart, and the component that connects all other Sephirot. In the same way the human heart pumps blood to fuel all functions of the body, the Tipareth powers the various parts of the Tree. In the diagram, notice how each Sephirah has a path leading back to the Tipareth, this is true of no other circle in the diagram. Below the Tipareth is Yesod, which represents the subconscious, and is connected to human sexuality. Take a moment to consider the world we live in and the constant subliminal sexual programming, from children's cartoons, to commercials, to TV shows and movies. Surely you've heard about "sex" being written in the clouds of Disney films, and unnecessary drawings of erections in men's pants in the backgrounds of a number of films from the same Disney studio. Sex sells and it occupies the mind, as you probably well know. To climb the pillars of the Tree of Life, you have to be able to rise above the sexual desires that are associated with this Sephirah, it is the one circle that many people are forever held down by. This belief associated with the specific circle can be paralleled to Priests within the Catholic Church, who are to maintain sexual abstinence. Below Yesod is Malkuth, which means kingdom. It represents the physical world, all of God's creation, which we exist within. Unlike the other nine Sephirot, it is an attribute of God that does not come from God directly, but instead from God's creation. It is the evidence of God's love and glory. Think of a beautiful natural setting, this is Malkuth.

In the diagram to the left, you can see how the Tree of Life is divided into four categories, commonly referred to as celestial worlds, or simply put, the 'Four Worlds'. In Reduction Gematria, 'Four Worlds' equates to 52, and in Reverse Reduction, it sums to 56, similar to the Gematriot of 'Tree of Life' and 'Etz haChayim'. At the top is Atziluth, which is the level representing God. Below that is Briah, where the Archangels dwell, the primary servants of God. This is the level of creation and creative energy. Below that is Yetzirah, where the creative energy takes form, and souls begin to exist. In this realm, Angels exist, what are heavenly beings ranking just below Archangels. The lowest realm, Assiah, is where the physical world exists, and where creation fully takes form. This is also the place where we exist. Kabbalah is a very complicated subject, and this description is only meant to begin to help you see the larger picture. Before transitioning away from the 'Four Worlds', I want to show you what is relevant about the name, in light of the Hebrew name for the 'Tree of Life', 'Etz haChayim'. Both titles have Gematria connecting to 'foundation', 'Orthodox' and 'Star of David'. Consider this diagram is the foundation of Kabbalah that is of extreme spiritual significance to many Orthodox Jews, who in Israel, are symbolized with the Star of David. At the same time, let us not forget the Tree of Life and the Star of David are both derived from the Flower of Life, the most sacred symbol in Sacred Geometry, as we learned earlier.

Etz haChayim = 5+20+26+8+1+3+8+1+25+9+13 = 119 (O)

Four Worlds = 21+12+6+9+4+12+9+15+23+8 = 119 (RO)

Star of David = 19+20+1+18 + 15+6 + 4+1+22+9+4 = 119 (O)

Orthodox = 15+18+20+8+15+4+15+24 = 119 (O)

Foundation = 6+15+21+14+4+1+20+9+15+14 = 119 (O)

Let us now transition to the spelling of 'Sephirot', what are the 10-circles we just familiarized ourselves with. The spelling of 'Sephirot' also connects with the Gematria of 'foundation', summing to 47, reminding of the year Zionist Israel was recognized as a nation, November 29, 1947, emphasis on '47, the 333rd day of the year. As we learned earlier, the words 'Elohim' and 'Judaism' in Hebrew also sum to 47, the number that embodies foundation and divinity. In addition to decoding 'Sephirot', let us also decode the singular, 'Sephirah', which sums to 48 in the Reduction method, matching the Ordinal value of 'Tree', and the year Israel officially became a nation, 1948. For another reminder, in Hebrew and in English, 'Freemason' also sums to 48, a very special number.

Sephirot = 1+5+7+8+9+9+6+2 = 47 (R)

Foundation = 6+6+3+5+4+1+2+9+6+5 = 47 (R)

Star of David = 1+2+1+9+6+6+4+1+4+9+4 = 47 (R)

Orthodox = 6+9+2+8+6+4+6+6 = 47 (R)

Sephirah = 1+5+7+8+9+9+1+8 = 48 (R)

Tree = 20+18+5+5 = 48 (O)

In the Septenary and Chaldean ciphers, which we became acquainted with in Chapter 4, 'Tree of Life' also equates to 48, as follows.

Tree of Life = 7+5+5+5+2+6+2+5+6+5 = 48 (Septenary)

Tree of Life = 4+2+5+5+7+8+3+1+8+5 = 48 (Chaldean)

On the subject of the number 48, it is the number 223 that is the 48th prime number. Consider that in the Tree of Life, there are 22 paths, connecting the 3-pillars, that contain the 10-Sephirot. As we covered in Chapter 4, the number 223 also connects to 'Masonic' and 'The Synagogue of Satan'. Just ahead, we will learn the darker half of the

Tree of Life, which is not about spiritual ascension, but instead, something much the opposite. It factors into the death of King James, who died after ruling for 22-years, over 3-kingdoms. Before we get there, let us examine one more fascinating point about the names 'Sephirah', as well as the alternate spelling, 'Sefirah'. Both spellings connect to the words 'ten' and 'five', as in the number of Sephirah / Sefirah, as well as the 5-books of the Torah, and the larger *Old Testament* the *Torah* exists within. As we decode, keep in mind the story of the Ten Commandments is from the *Torah* and *Old Testament*. Again, all the pieces of the puzzle are interrelated, and nothing in this study is arbitrary.

Sephirah = 8+4+2+1+9+9+8+1 = 42 (RR)

Sefirah = 8+4+3+9+9+8+1 = 42 (RR)

Sefirah = 1+5+6+9+9+1+8 = 39 (R)

Ten = 20+5+14 = 39 (O)

Ten = 7+22+13 = 42 (RO)

Five = 6+9+22+5 = 42 (O)

Five = 3+9+22+4 = 39 (RR, V22)

Even more, if you write out 'Ten Sephirot', it sums to 52 using the Septenary cipher, connecting to the Gematria of 'Kabbalah', 'Tree of Life' and 'Sephirot', as we began. As a reminder, these additional ciphers are complimentary to our base ciphers.

Ten Sephirot = 7+5+1+6+5+3+6+5+5+2+7 = 52 (Septenary)

At the same time, using Reverse Reduction, 'Ten Sephirot' sums to 58, connecting to the list of 'biblical' words equating to the number 58 we ended Chapter 2 with. We also concluded that same chapter with a list of words pertinent to 'Freemasonry' summing to the number 58. At this point, the parallels should be becoming clearer. And if you need to review, please feel inclined to go back and re-examine the lists of words having Gematria values of 58 from the end of Chapter 2.

Ten Sephirot = 7+4+4+8+4+2+1+9+9+3+7 = 58 (RR)

Biblical = 7+9+7+6+9+6+8+6 = 58 (RR)

Freemasonry = 6+9+5+5+4+1+1+6+5+9+7 = 58 (R)

On the subject of the *Bible*, there is a debate about *Genesis 3:22* in regards to if the verse, which mentions the *Tree of Life,* is indeed referencing the Kabbalistic Tree we are now learning about. I think it is safe to assume that this verse is in reference to the exact same Tree, in fact, I have zero doubt it is. Again, it is the belief of Kabbalists that the entire *Torah,* the first 5-books of the *Bible,* are encoded in the language of letters and numbers, and *Genesis* is the first of these 5-books. Knowing this, let us take a moment to examine both the King James Version of *Genesis 3:22*, as well as the New International Version. Then, let us prove that they are in reference to the Kabbalistic Tree. They are as follows.

Genesis 3:22 New International Version (NIV) And the Lord God said, "The man has now become like one of us, knowing good and evil. He must not be allowed to reach out his hand and take also from the tree of life and eat, and live forever."

Genesis 3:22 King James Version (KJV) And the Lord God said, Behold, the man is become as one of us, to know good and evil: and now, lest he put forth his hand, and take also of the tree of life, and eat, and live for ever:

To prove that these verses are in reference to the Kabbalistic Tree, we will decode the first sentence of each verse, having to do with knowing *"good and evil"*. Please notice that despite the different wordings, both verses sum to 322, not unlike the verse number, *Genesis 3:22*. And do not lose sight of the fact that the Tree has 3-pillars, connected by 22-paths. We will decode the (NIV) first, followed by the (KJV) second, using Reverse Reduction for both deciphers. Again, I encourage you to use *Gematrinator.com* to verify the math, and to make calculating longer phrases such as this a breeze.

And the Lord God said, "The man has now become like one of us, knowing good and evil =

8+4+5+7+1+4+6+3+9+5+2+3+5+8+8+9+5+7+1+4+5+8+4+1+8+8+4 +3+4+7+4+6+3+5+4+6+9+7+4+3+4+4+3+3+6+8+7+4+3+4+9+4+2+2+ 3+3+5+8+4+5+4+5+9+6 = 322

And the Lord God said, Behold, the man is become as one of us, to know good and evil =

8+4+5+7+1+4+6+3+9+5+2+3+5+8+8+9+5+7+4+1+3+6+5+7+1+4+5 +8+4+9+8+7+4+6 +3+5+4+8+8+3+4+4+3+3+6+8+7+3+7+4+3+4+2+3+3+5+8+4+5+4+5+ 9+6 = 322

The number decoded from both verses, 322, is not arbitrary, far from it. In fact, it is the number that connects the Jewish faith, the Christian faith, and the Islamic faith, which are considered the 'Abrahamic Religions', because they trace to the patriarch, 'Abraham', who as we learned in Chapter 1, has Gematria of 26, not unlike God. Not only does the number 322 connect the Abrahamic Religions, it also draws a straight parallel to the 'Ancient Mystery Religions' of Babylon, which includes Kabbalah. Even more, of the Ancient Mystery Religions, it is Kabbalah that is paramount. As we decode, please pay mind to the fact that 'Abrahamic' and 'Ancient Mystery' each sum to 187, matching the number of chapters in the *Torah* and the Hebrew Gematria value of 'Elohim'.

Abrahamic = 26+25+9+26+19+26+14+18+24 = 187 (187 chapters in *Torah*)

Religions = 9+22+15+18+20+18+12+13+8 = 135

Abrahamic Religions = 322 (RO)

Ancient = 26+13+24+18+22+13+7 = 123

Mystery = 14+2+8+7+22+9+2 = 64 (Ancient Mystery = 187, RO)

Religions = 9+22+15+18+20+18+12+13+8 = 135

Ancient Mystery Religions = 322 (RO)

Please also note that 'Ancient Mystery Religions' shares Gematria of 187.

Ancient Mystery Religions =

8+4+6+9+22+4+7+5+2+8+7+22+9+2+9+22+6+9+2+9+3+4+8 = 187 (RR, E22)

According to *Christianity.com*, the most recognized date for the first published *Gutenberg Bible* is March 22, 1457. In the United States that date is commonly written as 3/22, not unlike 322. According to *National Geographic,* another date credited in history books for the first publishing of the Gutenberg Bible, is February 23, 1455. That date can be written as 2/23, not unlike 223, what is the reflection of 322. Recall, numbers that mirror each other in this study are considered equals. Also, we learned in Chapter 4, both 'Masonic' and 'The Synagogue of Satan' have Gematria of 223, as well as the biblical name 'Philadelphia', the name of the church that receives the letter warning about 'The Synagogue of Satan'. On a related note, in more recent history, on March 22, 2017, the Tomb of Jesus was reopened in Israel, something we will cover ahead in the chapter on Christianity and the code. And possibly most relevant of all, regarding the number 223 and the *Bible,* the first verse of the entire text, where God speaks the world into existence, has encoded Gematria of 223, using the Reduction method.

Genesis 1:1 New International Version (NIV) In the beginning God created the heavens and the earth.

In the beginning God created the heavens and the earth = 9+5+2+8+5+2+5+7+9+5+5+9+5+7+7+6+4+3+9+5+1+2+5+4+2+8+5+8 +5+1+4+5+5+1 +1+5+4+2+8+5+5+1+9+2+8 = 223 (R)

For a bit more mathematical fun, we learned the number 223 is the 48th prime number, and the divisors of the number 33, sum to the number 48. The math for the sum of the divisors is as follows:

1+3+11+33 = 48. Related, notice how 'Good Book', a common nickname for the *Bible*, has Gematria of 33 as well as 48.

Good Book = 7+6+6+4+2+6+6+11 = 48 (R, K11)

Good Book = 2+3+3+5+7+3+3+7 = 33 (RR); Bible = 7+9+7+6+4 = 33 (RR)

Verse = 4+5+9+10+5 = 33 (R, S10); Genesis = 7+5+5+5+1+9+1 = 33 (R)

The name 'Good Book' also equates to 39 using Reduction and Chaldean Gematria, matching the number of books in the *Old Testament,* as well as the Gematria of 'Sefirah' and 'ten' as covered. And for good measure, notice how 'Good Book' also sums to the number 223 in Jewish Gematria, the cipher we learned of in Chapter 4.

Good Book = 7+50+50+4+2+50+50+10 = 223 (Jewish)

Think about what the Bible is. To quote the hip-hop album *Liquid Swords,* the *Bible* is "Basic Instructions Before Leaving Earth". In other words, it is full of wisdom to help you live right in your time on this planet, to help you choose good over evil, which is exactly what *Genesis 3:22* is in reference to. When you think about "good and evil", you probably also think about above (heaven) and below (hell), thus, *as above so below.*

With that said, *Genesis 3:22* is the 78th verse of the *Bible,* and here's why that matters.

Genesis = 7+5+14+5+19+9+19 = 78 (O)

As Above So Below = 8+8+8+7+3+5+4+8+3+7+4+6+3+4 = 78 (RR)

While we have not discussed the number 78 up to this point, it is of extreme importance. The names 'Jesuit' and 'Scottish Rite', both branches of Freemasonry, share this Gematria, which we will become more familiar with in the chapters ahead. *There's a reason records spin at 78 RPMs.*

Jesuit = 17+22+8+6+18+7 = 78 (RO)

Scottish Rite = 8+6+3+7+7+9+8+1+9+9+7+4 = 78 (RR)

As mentioned, these Masonic orders, while seemingly pure in intention and public image, have a darker half, that is in need of much exposure. At the tops of these very powerful entities, evil has been chosen over good, and this must be brought to light. Knowing that within these orders, Qabalah is being practiced, there is a darker half to the study as alluded to that we will now uncover. It goes by the name Qliphoth. The name 'Qliphoth' has Gematria of 48 in Reverse Reduction, factoring into the Ordinal values of 'Evil' and 'Tree', and a Reverse Sumerian value of 666, same as 'Genesis'. As we just learned, *Genesis 3:22* is in reference to the Kabbalistic Tree of Life, there can be no mistake about it when the code is applied. Thus, it makes sense that 'Qliphoth' and '*Genesis*' would share Gematria, as they do. Even more, the motto 'as above, so below' fits in as well.

Qliphoth = 1+6+9+2+10+3+7+10 = 48 (RR, H10)

As Above So Below = 1+1+1+2+6+4+5+1+6+2+5+3+6+5 = 48 (R)

Evil = 5+22+9+12 = 48 (O); Tree = 20+18+5+5 = 48 (O)

Qliphoth = 60+90+108+66+114+72+42+114 = 666 (Reverse Sumerian)

Genesis = 120+132+78+132+48+108+48 = 666 (Reverse Sumerian)

*Witchcraft = 138+54+120+18+48+18+108+6+36+120 = 666 (Sumerian)

What Qliphoth is used for is to obstruct holiness, or said otherwise, tarnish what is right. The reason for doing this is to gain power and have influence over others. The practitioners of Qliphoth aim to create distance from God, and in doing so acquire what can be explained as dark energy. This energy is then used to cast spells to change outcomes in the favor of the spell caster. Think about the word spell and its relation to language, in light of what we have learned. When you recognize that the mainstream media, each and everyday, has editors who are creating false stories, to instill fear and division, you can begin to come to terms with the real world application of Qliphoth. Think about how dark, depressing and draining the news media often is. Think about the impact the information (spells) being put out by these organizations is having on the people. For example, when I was a child, the late-80s and early-90s, there was a park I made many great memories in. It was bustling with children and everyday I played games there. Now, it is abandoned. It is empty. There are no children to be found.

Why? It is because of the fear mongering, because of the threats, because of the needless headlines that are based in lies and contrived horror stories, *spelled* out in black and white in papers and magazines, and broadcast on radios, televisions and smart phones.

Going forward, please understand that the New World Order, commonly referred to as the 'Illuminati', are the masters of these dark arts, what is Qliphoth. This is their tool to control us, to steer us, to divide us, and to keep us on the path of agenda they have setout for us. Because they operate from the dark, it is the light, which is knowledge, that can dispel their evil magic, and with this text, that is exactly what I aim to do. From Oklahoma City, to 9/11, to the Boston Marathon Bombing, to Sandy Hook, to the Route 91 Harvest Festival shooting in Las Vegas, plus so much more, these are the acts of Qliphoth, and this is what the people of the world must know. For good measure, let us decode the words 'Illuminati' and 'Freemason', keeping in mind that in Hebrew, 'Freemason' also equates to 48.

Illuminati = 9+3+3+3+4+9+5+1+2+9 = 48 (R)

Freemason = 3+9+4+4+5+8+8+3+4 = 48 (RR)

מַסוֹן = 13+15+6+14 = 48 (Freemason in Hebrew Ordinal)

As we wind down, there are a few other interesting notes about Kabbalah that you should be aware of. According to Kabbalists we are still living in the biblical times, they never ended. Thus, the 'flood' is still taking place. Think about this in light of constant news programming of rising oceans and global warming. In the Ordinal method, 'flood' sums to 52, and when we arrive at the chapter on weather warfare by the numbers, we'll learn how important this Kabbalistic number is to "unnatural flooding" throughout history, that has been blamed on mother nature, going back to 1952, with the Lynmouth Flood of August 15 and 16 that year. Also interesting, many Kabbalists contend that God did not kick Adam and Eve out of the Garden of Eden, but instead, Adam and Eve removed God from the Garden by eating from the forbidden tree, at the behest of the serpent. Also interesting, according to Kabbalah, God is both male and female, like the masculine and feminine parts of the Tree of Life we learned about earlier. Consider that in the same media that needlessly casts fear on the masses, there is now an agenda to push confusion about human sexuality, through what has been coined "transgender". Being someone who works with youth, I do see the impact this news programming has had on the minds of many young people, who are easily influenced by what is shown on television.

To conclude our learning on this subject, there are those who contend Kabbalah is extremely dangerous, even when it is used by the person who seeks spiritual ascension, because it is a practice with the aim of achieving Godliness, which goes against the wishes of God (Elohim / YHWH), as expressed in *Genesis* and quite clearly in verse 3:22, the one we carefully examined, and prior to that, in *Genesis 2:16*. Regarding 2:16, notice the verse is much like the number 216, what is the product of 6x6x6, something like the Gematria of *Genesis,* equating to 666.

Genesis 2:16-17 New International Version (NIV) 16 And the Lord God commanded the man, "You are free to eat from any tree in the garden; 17 but you must not eat from the tree of the knowledge of good and evil, for when you eat from it you will certainly die."

There are some *Bible* researchers who believe this story is alluding to sex. This is because after eating from the Tree, Adam and Eve become conscious of their naked bodies for the first time, and God punishes Eve by making her pregnant and to endure terrible labor pains. With sex in mind, consider that Adam and Eve are not to eat from the Tree in the middle of the garden, and in the middle of the Tree of Life, is Yesod, which represents the genitals, and which gives man the ability to procreate, similar to how God creates life. Further, recall how we learned XXX means 666 and it is this number that is often used in regards to sexually explicit material. Even more, the word 'sex' has Gematria of 48 matching 'Tree', as well as 33, matching *Genesis* and *Bible.*

Sex = 19+5+24 = 48 (O); Sex = 8+22+3 = 33 (RO)

In the *Bible,* as mentioned, it is the serpent that deceives Adam and Eve, persuading them to eat the forbidden fruit, which results in their banishment. Notice it is *Genesis 3:4* where the serpent begins to persuade Eve, who then eats from the tree, before feeding the same fruit to Adam. That verse follows.

Genesis 3:4-5 New International Version (NIV) "You will not certainly die," the serpent said to the woman. 5 "For God knows that when you eat from it your eyes will be opened, and you will be like God, knowing good and evil.

It is extremely fascinating that the verse begins with *Genesis 3:4* when you apply the Gematria code to the terms 'Adam and Eve', 'disobey' and 'serpent'. Each equates to a numerical value of 34 as follows.

Adam and Eve = 1+4+1+4+1+5+4+5+4+5 = 34 (R)

105

Disobey = 4+9+1+6+2+5+7 = 34 (R); Serpent = 1+5+9+7+5+5+2 = 34 (R)

Considering that the Tree of Life, which they ate from, also relates to Kabbalah, which relates to letters, numbers, and language, it is equally as fascinating that 'Hebrew', 'Latin', and 'English' equate to the number 34 just as well.

Hebrew = 8+5+2+9+5+5 = 34 (R); Latin = 6+8+7+9+4 = 34 (RR)

English = 4+4+2+6+9+8+1 = 34 (RR)

Adding to the intrigue, the fact that it is Genesis 3:5 that speaks about opening the eyes, you should be reminded that 'eye' sums to 35 (Eye = 5+25+5 = 35). On the subject, I hope you're finding this knowledge to be eye opening. And in case you're wondering, I do not think we are disobeying God by learning this code. If you use it for the dark side however, what is evil, as the tyrants do, then we'll let God be the judge. That said, I imagine your intention, as the reader of this text, is the same as mine, which is to increase knowledge, for the sake of overcoming. If so, that is just, righteous, and necessary.

*In the *Torah*, there are 62 verses mentioning the Garden of Eden. 'Torah' and 'Elohim' sum to 62 in Ordinal; 'Garden of Eden' sums to 62 in Reduction

NINE

CHAPTER

◄∞►

Greeks, Geometry, Gematria & the Jesus Isopsephy Riddle

"There is geometry in the humming of the strings; there is music in the spacing of the spheres." "Everything is arranged according to number and mathematical shape."

"Geometry is knowledge of the eternally existent." "Numbers rule the universe." – Pythagoras

"Geometry will draw the soul toward truth and create the spirit of philosophy."

"Numbers are the highest degree of knowledge. It is knowledge itself."

"Geometry existed before creation."

– Plato

As we have learned, the Greeks, studying the civilizations that came before them, including the Egyptians, Chaldeans, Babylonians, Sumerians, and Far East, came to have a deep appreciation for mathematics. As a result, Ancient Greece built a culture and empire centered on numbers where math became the basis for philosophy, science, spirituality, art, architecture, music and language. Again, I will recommend the 1959 Disney cartoon, *Donald in Mathmagic Land,* for an intuitive presentation of the Greeks, Geometry and culture. The only thing the short animated feature leaves out is Gematria, and we know why... Had Disney educated on this matter, it would have become clear why the flick was released in '59, as the year pays homage to the Pythagoreans, who were secretive, and considered cultish, similar to Freemasonry. In case you're not aware, Walt Disney was a member of the fraternal organization, and in the language of Gematria, both 'Pythagorean' and 'Freemasonry' equate to 59, and in Hebrew, 'Freemasonry' (מינובה םייׁשפוחה) also sums to 59, just another of many overlaps between English and Hebrew, two languages, having parallels to the Greeks, that both share a mathematical basis. Regarding 59, it is the 17th prime number, and in the chapter ahead on Masonry, you will learn why the Premier Grand Lodge, beginning the era of modern Freemasonry, was opened in the year 1717; think 'Mason', think 'God'. On the subject, it was

Euclid, the Greek, the "Father of Geometry", who documented in his most remembered work, *Elements,* the first record of prime numbers, in 300 BCE.

Pythagorean = 2+2+7+10+8+2+3+9+4+8+4 = 59 (RR, H10)

Freemasonry = 3+9+4+4+5+8+8+3+4+9+2 = 59 (RR)

םייׁשפוחה מינובה = 5+2+6+5+1+4+5+8+6+8+3+1+1+4 = 59 (Hebrew Reduction)

Much of the Grecian mathematical focus was due to the achievements of Pythagoras and Plato as well as the numerous others who followed in their footsteps, including Euclid, who were

108

known as Pythagoreans and Platonists respectively. To this very day the discoveries of Ancient Greece are taught in math classrooms across the world. As we break down 'Greece', 'Platonism' and 'Foundation', pay mind to the Gematria of 119. In numerology terms, 119 breaks down to 1+1+9 is 11, the master number, fitting for the master Grecian teachers, at least according to history books.

As is no secret to many, history likes to give credit to the white man, when it is not always the credit of the white race.

Greece = 20+9+22+22+24+22 = 119 (RO)

Platonism = 16+12+1+20+15+14+9+19+13 = 119 (O)

Foundation = 6+15+21+14+4+1+20+9+15+14 = 119 (O)

At the same time, please know the 'Ancient Mystery Religions', having Gematria of 119, which includes Kabbalah, are very numbers oriented, because for as long as time, numbers have been associated with The Creator. As we learned last chapter, the Hebrew name for the Tree of Life, 'Etz haChayim', shares Ordinal Gematria of 119 as well. I bring this point up because both Pythagoras and Plato were well studied in the mysticism of Kabbalah, having learned the knowledge in Egypt. According to Masonic author Manly P. Hall, in his work *Crate Repoa, or Initiations to the Ancient Mysteries of the Priest of Egypt*, Plato received his Rites of Isis and Osiris in Egypt at the very specific age of 47-years, the number symbolizing 'time' and 'foundation', as covered. This same Egyptian fraternity of knowledge was in the mold of modern Freemasonry. Let us not forget that it was Manly P. Hall who received

his 33rd ° from the Scottish Rite of Freemasonry, exactly 47-years after publishing his most remembered work, *The Secret Teachings of All Ages*, a title that ties to the number 47 itself. We'll get to it in the chapters ahead, and what Manly P. Hall forgot to teach his

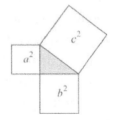

readers that he very clearly knew about, and neglected intentionally. Just as forthcoming as Manly appeared, he was equally as secretive. Tis the nature of a man who has taken oaths to contain secrets, as a Mason does.

Ancient Mystery Religions =

1+5+3+9+5+5+2+4+7+1+2+5+9+7+9+5+3+9+7+9+6+5+1   = 119

Of the many lessons from the Greek's still with us, one most people know by name is the *Pythagorean Theorem*, or $a^2 +$

$b^2 = c^2$, often used to find the length of an unknown side of a right triangle; another is Pi, 3.14, what is used to solve for the circumference and area of a circle; a third is Phi, 1.61, the Golden Ratio, said to be the fingerprint of God and aesthetically pleasing to the human eye when used in artwork, as it has from the time of Phidias, the Greek sculptor, up to the present. Not by chance, the word 'aesthetics' has Reverse Ordinal Gematria of 161, not unlike 1.61.

Aesthetics = 26+22+8+7+19+22+7+18+24+8 = 161 (RO)

Of the most known symbols where Phi reveals itself, is the Pentagram. Many people mistake this symbol with evil, when in fact, it is yet another object from Sacred Geometry that pertains to spiritual uplift, unless it is inverted, meaning flipped upside down. So long as the point is up, the Pentagram has a positive vibration. To the left, please notice the illustration, where the top point represents spirit, then moving clockwise, the next point water, then fire, then earth, then air. As you'll recall from the chapter on Sacred Geometry, these same elements pertain to the Platonic Solids, the only five known three-dimensional shapes with perfect geometric symmetry, taught about by Pythagoras and written about by Plato as well as Euclid, thus the name Platonic, and thus the reason Euclid's most remembered work is titled *Elements*. For review, the five 3-D shapes are the 4-sided Tetrahedron (fire), 6-sided Cube (earth), 8-sided Octahedron (air), 12-sided Icosahedron (water), and 20-sided Dodecahedron (energy / ether / spirit).

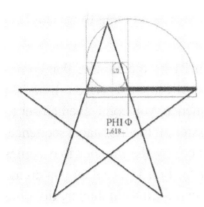

As for how the Pentagram relates to Phi, please use the image shown to the left. The ratio of the lines that make up each of the five sides of the inner pentagon, when compared with the remainder of the lines extending beyond the pentagon to each point, is that of 1.618, what is Phi. In the same Disney cartoon from '59, *Donald in Mathmagic Land,* it does a wonderful job of bringing this relationship to life. As for the spiral shown in the illustration, that is the visualization of the Golden Ratio, what is also Phi. Let us now carefully examine this spiral, considered to be "God's mathematical spiral", or "God's thumb print", connecting it to the Fibonacci sequence, which we learned of earlier, what is also known as "God's mathematical sequence".

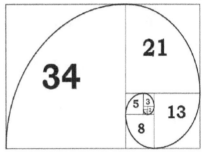

Recall the Fibonacci sequence is introduced in the Hollywood film *Pi*, in the same scene where the viewer is introduced to Gematria and Kabbalah. Recall further that 'Fibonacci' also shares Gematria with 'God'.

Please review if need be. The wise person will read this text at least twice, as there is much knowledge to be learned and memorized. The even wiser person will take notes as they read.

To the right is a clearer illustration of the same spiral, the Golden Ratio, shown in the drawing above of the Pentagram that emphasizes the relationship with Phi. As you can see, the numbers within the spiral are that of the Fibonacci sequence; they are 1, 1, 2, 3, 5, 8, 13, 21, 34... and if it continued on, the following numbers would be 55, 89, 144, 233, 377, 610, 987, and so on to infinity. It is dividing these numbers that creates the parallel to Phi.

Beginning with dividing the number 21 by the number that comes before it, 13, you get an approximation of Phi, 1.61. If you divide 34 by 21, the next two numbers in the sequence, you come even closer to the true ratio for Phi. With each progression of the Fibonacci sequence, by dividing a number from the sequence, by the number that comes before it, you approach the true number for Phi. Thus, when you divide 233 by 144, you will be closer to the true ratio for Phi than by dividing 144 by 89. Of course that also means that if you divide 377 by 233, you'll be closer to Phi than by dividing 233 by 144.

Again, with each progression, you approach the true Phi, I want to make sure the point is abundantly clear, so I apologize for the redundancy if you got it the first time.

Earlier I mentioned Stephen Curry of the Golden State Warriors, who has a Pi Day birthday, March 14, and how we will get to the Pi rituals in his championship season, 2016-17 (in light of 2016, keep in mind Pi is the 16th letter of the Greek alphabet). That is still ahead, but another related point arises now. In that same season, his Golden State Warriors acquired David West, another star of the league. Shortly after joining the Warriors, West received a new tattoo on his right shoulder, that of the Golden Ratio, the same spiral we just uncovered that connects to Phi (both Pi and Phi begin with 'p', what is the 16th letter of the English alphabet). Think about it, a Golden Ratio, to join the Golden State Warriors, in 2016, emphasis on '16. Not by chance, the Warriors would go 16-1 in the playoffs, winning the championship, not unlike Phi, 1.61. Making matters even more comical, it was the 71st

112

season of the NBA. As we learned in Chapter 4, the word 'God' sums to 71 in English Extend Gematria, just as the name 'Zeus', the Greek God, sums to 71 in Ordinal Gematria (the Greeks are credited with the discovery of Phi and Phi is connected to God). Let us not lose sight of the fact that this ratio is connected to God because of how it shows up in nature, from the Milky Way Galaxy, to hurricanes, to spiral seeds, to the cochlea of human ears (and most mammals), to the anatomy of the human body, to DNA molecules, to seashells, to a ram's horns, to sea-horse tails, to fern leaves, to waves breaking on the beach, to tornados, to whirlpools, to sunflowers, to daisies, to dandelions, and more. Even better, the word 'tattoo' sums to 71 in Reverse Ordinal, and here we are talking about David West's tattoo, which foretold the scripted 71st NBA season for the Golden State Warriors, that he was no doubt made to put on his body after joining the team. As you'll learn, these men are branded no different than cattle, and despite high salaries, they aren't much different than slaves.

Tattoo = 7+26+7+7+12+12 = 71 (RO)

Zeus = 26+5+21+19 = 71 (O)

God = 7+60+4 = 71 (English Extended)

By knowing the code, the comedy of rigged sports can provide many laughs. Consider that in that same 2016 season, where the Warriors won their 5th NBA Championship, and the 25th overall championship for the Western Conference, where 25 has a square root of 5, it paired rather well with the 5-sided Pentagram, that the Golden Ratio is associated with. Equally as intriguing, 'Golden Ratio' and 'NBA Finals', as well as the word 'Golden' alone, have much in common in Gematria. When you factor in the Kabbalah ciphers we learned in Chapter 4, the name 'West' also equates.

Golden Ratio = 7+6+3+4+5+5+9+1+2+9+6 = 57 (R)

The NBA Finals = 2+8+5+5+2+1+6+9+5+1+3+10 = 57 (R, S10)

NBA Finals = 4+7+8 + 3+9+4+8+6+8 = 57 (RR)

Golden = 7+15+12+4+5+14 = 57 (O)

West = 3+25+5+24 = 57 (ALW Kabbalah) (David West, player with Tattoo)

Also important, when David West signed with the Warriors and received the tattoo, he was at the tail end of being 35-years-old. Notice the product of 5x7 is 35. We are multiplying 5x7 because those are the numerical digits in the relevant words we just decoded, having Gematria of 57. You'll notice how number 35 connects with the name 'David West' as well as 'tattoo', for one last riddle on the subject for the time being. Ahead you'll learn what number 35 has to do with the real 'King James' and his death, in light of the Warriors defeating LeBron James, aka *King James,* and West's championship teammate for the 2016-17 season, Kevin Durant, who wears number 35.

David West = 4+1+4+9+4+5+5+1+2 = 35 (R)

Tattoo = 7+8+7+7+3+3 = 35 (RR)

Coming back to the Pentagram, the illustration to the left shows the degrees of the angles that are formed. You'll notice the Pentagram that is within the larger Pentagon that is surrounded by a circle creates 5-Golden Gnomon triangles, which we were introduced to in Chapter 2. The degrees on those respective triangles are two acute 36-degree angles and one obtuse 108-degree angle. For a reminder of the significance of the Gematria of the word 'Geometry', I want to decode the word so as to compare how it syncs with these angles from this very important geometric shape.

Geometry = 7+5+15+13+5+20+18+25 = 108 (O)

114

Geometry = 20+22+12+14+22+7+9+2 = 108 (RO)

Geometry = 7+5+6+4+5+2+9+7 = 45 (R)

Geometry = 2+4+3+5+4+7+9+2 = 36 (RR)

*Golden   State   Warriors   =
7+6+3+4+5+5+10+2+1+2+5+5+1+9+9+9+6+9+10 = 108 (R, S10)

You'll notice, the word Geometry equates to 108 forwards and backwards, as well as 36 in Reverse Reduction, matching the interior angles of the triangle in focus. As we learned in Chapter 2, the Golden Gnomon was considered a sacred object to Pythagoras, largely because of its relationship with the Pentagram, as shown. The other classification of triangle sacred to Pythagoras was a 'Golden Triangle', where the Pentagram forms 5 of these, each extending from the Pentagon in the middle, where the base of each Golden Triangle extends from the five sides of the Pentagon. What makes the Golden Triangle special is that the ratio of the hypotenuse to the base, creates Phi. In Reduction Gematria,

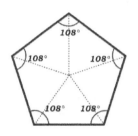

'Golden Triangle' sums to 71, also corresponding with the Warriors very geometric 71st season. I suppose I should also mention that 'Pentagon', in Reverse Ordinal, sums to 124, and David West's birthday, August 29, is the 241st day of the year, leaving 124-days remaining. Think about it, the 5-sided object, in the middle of a Pentagram, where each interior angle of the object sums to 108-degrees, pairs ever so nicely with the 'Golden State Warriors' 5th championship season, don't you think?

Pentagon = 11+22+13+7+26+20+12+13 = 124 (RO)

Golden Triangle = 7+6+3+4+5+5 + 2+9+9+1+5+7+3+5 = 71 (R)

As you can gather, these things are far beyond coincidental. And for a reminder, Sacred Geometry, which these shapes belong to, is the bridge between mathematics and the spiritual, having the underlying belief that God is the master mathematician who has constructed our reality using universal patterns that are geometric in nature. This is where the tie in comes with Kabbalah, the spiritual belief that God created the world with language, by merging the letter with the number. As we can now appreciate, these respective belief systems and the totality of this knowledge is truly part of one larger system, hidden within the English language, and being used ritualistically, on a daily basis, from the rigging of sports, to the contriving of news headlines, all for the sake of playing God over the masses, by a very dishonest, nefarious and arrogant group of elitists, who almost exclusively are followers of the *Talmud*, dating back to Babylon. Because these spiritual practices are being used this way, it does not mean you should discount the knowledge, but instead you should appreciate it, and find reason in why people would go to the lengths that they are. As Sun Tzu taught, *know your enemy.*

Let us now transition to the topic of Isopsephy, the Greek word for Gematria. Just as a reminder, when the coding and encoding of words is practiced within Hebrew, it is known as Gematria, and when practiced within Greek, it is Isopsephy. Also recall, in Chapter 3, we learned how *Revelation 13:18*, about the number of the beast, the number of a man, was a Greek Isopsephy riddle, truly pointing to the nature of humanity, and how the Greeks are responsible for the *New Testament* as well as *Revelation*, thus why the verse is written as it is. We also learned how both 'humanity' and 'Isopsephy' equate to 666, the same number riddled in *Revelation 13:18.* In the time of Pythagoras, he taught Isopsephy amongst a list of other related topics, including mathematics and knowledge of the stars above, after studying in the biblical lands. Where he taught was known as the School at Croton, on the eastern coast of Italy. After Pythagoras, Plato carried on the same tradition, teaching at what is recognized as the world's first university, Plato's Academy at Athens. Above the door to the school, it was inscribed, "Let no man ignorant of geometry enter here." Just the same as at Pythagoras's school in Croton, a student would have to have basic understanding of Geometry and the stars above to attend. Recall from Chapter 2, we learned the relationship between the word 'Geometry' and our nearest star, the sun. In case you have forgotten, it is said that the diameter of the sun is the same as the diameter of 108-earths, and the distance from the earth to the sun, is the same as the diameter of 108-suns. At the same time, from the earth to the moon, is said to be the diameter of 108-moons. These calculations also trace back to the Greeks; history states the men who followed in the footsteps of Pythagoras and Plato achieved them. As for that motto above the door of Plato's academy, let us decode and see how it connects to the word 'mathematics' alone.

Let no man ignorant of geometry enter here =

3+5+2+5+6+4+1+5+9+7+5+6+9+1+5+2+6+6+7+5+6+4+5+2+9+ 7+5+5+2+5+9+8+5+9+5 = 185 (R)

Mathematics = 14+26+7+19+22+14+26+7+18+24+8 = 185 (RO)

While I personally find the Ordinal value of 'mathematics' to be more interesting, what is the value of 112, similar to 1+1 = 2, the value of 185 is also noteworthy. Within the human body, we are made of 18.5% carbon, what is considered the "God element". Perhaps this is the reason for the encoding, or perhaps it has entirely to do with Plato's remembered quote, on the world's first university, at least as is remembered by history. Today, in math classrooms across the world, you can find this same motto stapled to walls on posters and plaques, but how many of these same teachers know about the numbers behind the letters?

For an example of Greek Isopsephy most English speaking people will be able to interpret and understand, let's read a section of the *Sibylline Oracles,* a well known collection of spoken utterances from the Greek Sibyls, those once believed to receive prophecy from the Greek Gods. The translated words that follow were originally transcribed using the Greek alphabet, around 150 CE, nearly 1,000 years after the creation of the Greek alphabet.

"When the virgin shall give birth to the Word of God the Most High, she shall give to the Word a Name, and from the east a star will shine in the midst of day gleaming down from heaven above proclaiming to mortal men a great sign. Yes, then shall the Son of the Great God come to men, clothed in flesh like mortals on earth. He has four vowels and in him, twofold the consonants ... and now I will declare to you the whole number ... eight monads, and to these as many decads, and eight hundreds his name will show."

First, notice the emphasis on the number 8. As we learned, this is a number symbolizing God's infiniteness (∞) and power and as you can clearly read, God is part of the equation. As you might be able to gather, the passage is in regards to Jesus, or in Greek, Iēsous, not far off from Zeus, the greatest Greek God of all. Some historians claim the words were spoken before the birth of Jesus Christ, prior to being recorded in the *Sibylline Oracles*. Other historians claim just the opposite, that these prophecies were contrived after the fact, as mentioned, near 150 CE. No matter, the purpose of our examination is to understand the ancient Greek practice of Isopsephy, or numerical riddle behind the written word. To make sense of what is posed in this example, you must know the Greek alphabet is an alphanumeric system, meaning letters are used to make sounds for the creation of spoken and written words, while also doubling as numbers for counting, no different than Hebrew, or as you now know, English. In total, the Greek alphabet is 24-letters, thus 24-numbers in length. The first set of 8 letters represent numbers 1 through 9 (with 6 being skipped), what are known as monads. The second set of 8 letters represent the numbers 10 through 80, what are known as decads; and the final set of 8 letters represent the numbers 100 through 800, or the hundreds, as referred to in the Isopsephy riddle. If you're paying attention, that means the values for 6, 90 and 900 are missing. To make up for the discrepancy, the Isopsephy system adds the letters Digamma (later Stigma) for 6 (w); Koppa for 90 (q); and Sampi for 900 (ts). For clarity, see the chart:

Greek Letter	Name	Numerical Value	Transliteration
A α	alpha	1	a
B β	beta	2	b
Γ γ	gamma	3	g
Δ δ	delta	4	d
E ε	epsilon	5	e
Z ζ	zeta	7	z
H η	eta	8	ē
Θ θ	theta	9	th
I ι	iota	10	i
K κ	kappa	20	k
Λ λ	lambda	30	l
M μ	mu	40	m
N ν	nu	50	n
Ξ ξ	xi	60	x
O o	omicron	70	o
Π π	pi	80	p
P ρ	rho	100	r
Σ σ/ς	sigma	200	s
T τ	tau	300	t
Y υ	upsilon	400	y
Φ φ	phi	500	ph
X χ	chi	600	ch
Ψ ψ	psi	700	ps
Ω ω	omega	800	ō
F ς	Digamma (Stigma)	6	w
Ϙ	Koppa	90	q
ϡ	Sampi	900	ts

In the *Sibylline Oracles* riddle it says the value of the name when calculated will sum to 8 monads, which are 8 ones. Then it says the same amount of decads, which are the tens, implying 80. Then last, 8 hundreds, which are 800. Thus it is 8+80+800 = 888. Using Isopsephy, the name for Jesus in Greek, Iēsous, has a value of 888, and also fulfills the other requirements mentioned, being a name made of 4 vowels and 2 consonants (Vowels: I, ē, o, u; Consonants: s, s), being of a virgin birth, and being born under a star of a great sign. Thus the Isopsephy problem can be solved with evidence (*Holy Bible*), and mathematically, with careful computation. The mathematics for calculating the name Iēsous to 888, using the chart, are as follows.

Iēsous = iota + eta + sigma + omicron + upsilon + sigma = 888
Iēsous = 10+8+200+70+400+200 = 888

For this example, there are multiple fascinating aspects about the name Iēsous having a value of 888 in Greek Isopsephy beyond what we have already learned about the digit 8. First, the number 888 is symbolic of the numerical structure of the Greek alphabet, broken into three sections of 8; 8-monads; 8-decads; 8-hundreds. Fittingly, this system is known as the Greek Ionic System, dating back to the 8th Century BCE. Further, when you duplicate and triplicate a digit in numerology, such as 8 becoming 88 and 888, you magnify the power of the qualities of the number with each replication. In terms of multiplying the symbolism of power and the infinite (8 to 888), consider this is for the name of the Son of God; God being a figure that is omnipotent, omnipresent, and everlasting in our understanding, something greater than the sum of all other things, having no equal. Thus the number 888 is appropriate as a numerical representation for the name of the Son of God, Iēsous, in a language that is based in numerical meaning, and which was created as tribute to God, in the same way Hebrew was, according to Kabbalah. Let us not forget that in Hebrew, 'YHWH' sums to 26, and in English, 'God' does too, which are both numbers breaking down to the number 8 as well (26 = 2+6 = 8).

Even deeper, in numerology practice, 888 becomes 8+8+8 = 24, and 24 = 2+4 = 6. God's sun, the keeper of time for earth, who dies and resurrects each day, seemingly in infinite repetition, is measured in 24-

hour cycles, and the number 6 alone is said to be the number of perfection as well as the number of man. Very quickly, let us decode 'the sun', using Reduction Gematria.

The Sun = 2+8+5+1+3+5 = 24 (R) (24-hours in a day) (24-letters in Greek)

Shamash = 1+8+1+4+1+1+8 = 24 (R) (*Ancient Babylonian Sun God)

If you are well read, you have likely crossed the opinion Jesus is an allegory for the sun and the sun's spiritual energy, which is love, which makes all life possible, encapsulated in the story of a mortal man, God's Son. Very quickly, let us examine the symmetrical Gematria of 'love', and how it corresponds with 'sun'.

Sun = 19+21+14 = 54 (O); Horus = 19+12+9+6+8 = 54 (RO)

Love = 12+15+22+5 = 54 (O); Love = 15+12+5+22 = 54 (RO)

This theory of Jesus as the sun in the sky becomes all the more fascinating when you decode the names into numbers. Before decoding, please consider the two various spellings for the word 'sun' and 'son'.

The Sun = 2+8+5+10+3+5 = 33 (R, S10)

God's Son = 2+3+5+8+8+3+4 = 33 (RR)

Jehovah = 1+5+8+6+4+1+8 = 33 (R)

Saviour = 1+1+4+9+6+3+9 = 33 (R) (Without 'u', it sums to 30, the age his ministry began)

Son = 8+12+13 = 33 (RO); Name = 13+1+14+5 = 33 (O)

As we have covered earlier, 'Bible', 'Good Book', 'Gospels' and 'Sunday' all share Gematria of 33 as well. Let us also decode 'Galilee', where Jesus began his ministry, as well as the word 'preach'. If you research, you'll find the Sea of Galilee is said to have a circumference of 33-miles, matching its Gematria, and similar to the age at which

Jesus was crucified. Consider Jesus was said to be able to walk on water, not unlike the reflection of the sun.

Galilee = 7+1+3+9+3+5+5 = 33 (R); Preach = 7+9+5+1+3+8 = 33 (R)

Related, think of the miracles Jesus performed with fish. We'll come back to this topic when we finish with the encoding of the number 33 in regards to the Son of God, and Jesus Christ as a metaphor for the sun in the sky.

Fish = 6+9+10+8 = 33 (R, S10)

In Christian prayer it is common to finish by saying the word 'Amen'. This word is used to 'bless' the subject of the prayer. Fittingly, both words also equate to this sacred number, 33, connecting to we 'people' as well. Please recall that each of us have 33-vertebrae in our back, and the words 'people' and 'person' equate to 33, as does the derogatory term 'goyim', used by followers of the *Talmud,* what is Rabbinic Judaism.

Amen = 1+13+5+14 = 33 (O); Bless = 7+6+4+8+8 = 33 (RR)

To draw a deeper parallel to Jesus Christ and the sun above, consider the Romans conquered Greece in the year 146 BCE. Again, it was the Greek's who wrote the *New Testament*, where one of the most remembered verses in regards to Jesus Christ is *John 14:6.* That verse is as follows.

John 14:6 New International Version (NIV) Jesus answered, "I am the way and the truth and the life. No one comes to the Father except through me."

In Reverse Ordinal Gematria, 'Jesus Christ' sums to 146, as does 'Capricorn', the astrological sign taking place when Christians celebrate the birthday of Jesus Christ across the world. The celebration comes on December 25, after the sun's duration in the sky begins to increase, coming just days after the Winter Solstice in the northern hemisphere, which is measured by the 'Tropic of Cancer', also summing to 146

Jesus Christ = 17+22+8+6+8+24+19+9+18+8+7 = 146 (RO)

Capricorn = 24+26+11+9+18+24+12+9+13 = 146 (RO)

Tropic of Cancer = 20+18+15+16+9+3+15+6+3+1+14+3+5+18 = 146 (O)

Time = 71+23+41+11 = 146 (Primes)

Think about the infiniteness of the sun, at least seemingly to we mortal souls. Again, in Greek Isopsephy, the name of Jesus Christ symbolizes the infinite, with the repeating symbolism of 888. Mathematically 12 can divide that number, which when divided by 12 equates to 74 (888 / 12 = 74; 74x12 = 888). For a moment, consider Jesus and his 12-disciples. You might have heard before Jesus is a metaphor for the sun and the 12 constellations of the Zodiac. In terms of all of the numbers related to Jesus Christ in English, the number 74 is one of the most special. In the *Bible*, the word 'stake' and 'crucify' are used exactly 74 times. Consider the crucifix, which is a cross, has also been used historically to symbolize the seasons, which are in direct relation to the sun.

Jesus = 10+5+19+21+19 = 74 (O); Cross = 3+18+15+19+19 = 74 (O)

Ankh = 26+13+16+19 = 74 (RO) (Egyptian word for cross)

Gospel = 7+15+19+16+5+12 = 74 (O)

Preacher = 16+18+5+1+3+8+5+18 = 74 (O)

Messiah = 13+5+19+19+9+1+8 = 74 (O)

Jewish = 10+5+23+9+19+8 = 74 (O) (Jesus said to be a Jew)

Roman = 9+12+14+26+13 = 74 (RO) (Put to death by Romans)

Killing = 11+9+12+12+9+14+7 = 74 (RO) (A 'Cross' is for 'killing')

Christianity = 3+8+9+9+10+2+9+1+5+9+2+7 = 74 (R, S10)

Jesus Christ = 8+4+8+6+8+6+1+9+9+8+7 = 74 (RR)

Heavens = 8+5+1+22+5+14+19 = 74 (O)

*Fruit = 6+18+21+9+20 = 74 (O) *(Recall the Fruit of Life and the 13-cirlces)*

*Muhammad = 13+21+8+1+13+13+1+4 = 74 (O) (Islamic Prophet after Jesus)

*Lucifer = 12+21+3+9+6+5+18 = 74 (O) (KJV, adversary to Jesus)

Do not forget that the words 'Masonic', 'English' and 'Gematria' all have Ordinal values of 74 too. Connecting with the Gematria of 74 is how the *New Testament* begins with the 42-generations to Jesus, a very specific number to Jesus Christ, the savior, himself.

Forty-Two = 21+12+9+7+2+7+4+12 = 74 (RO)

Let us again decode the significance of 42, which we briefly covered earlier. Do not forget that the Christian belief is Jesus died for man's sins. And in case you are not aware, there is a debate over the proper way to spell 'savior', either having a 'u', or without, which stems from the King James Bible, just like the spelling of 'forty' without the letter 'u'. What's interesting in Gematria terms is both spellings take us to 42.

New Testament = 5+5+5+2+5+1+2+1+4+5+5+2 = 42 (R)

Nazareth = 4+8+1+8+9+4+7+1 = 42 (RR)

Saviour = 10+1+4+9+6+3+9 = 42 (R, S10)

Savior = 8+8+5+9+3+9 = 42 (RR); Sin = 19+9+14 = 42 (O)

The number 42 is one we will uncover more about, but for now, please also recognize how it links with the number 26, representing God, as we learned to begin this journey. For the record, 'chain' and 'link' also share Gematria of 26, and as they say, all things are connected. I would contend that is because of the way 'God' has constructed this world.

Twenty-Six = 2+5+5+5+2+7+1+9+6 = 42

As for the celebrated birthday of Jesus Christ, there is something pertinent we must also address. First know the Gematria of 'birthday' is 42 in Reduction.

Birthday = 2+9+9+2+8+4+1+7 = 42 (R)

Historically, before Christianity existed, the Pagans would celebrate December 25 as the birthday of the 'Solar Man'. Manly P. Hall has done good work on this subject, sharing how the Christian Church in history changed the birthday of Jesus to this date as a means of luring Pagans and solstice worshipers into the Christian Church. As many *Bible* historians will tell you, the true birthday of Jesus Christ is not in the dead of winter, but the 'summer' when the sun's love is most warmly felt. In light of this Pagan celebration of the 'Solar Man', let us decode the name, as well as terms that are clearly relevant to Jesus, such as 'God's Son', 'Nazareth', 'Gospels', and 'Crucifix'. As we decode, do not forget that the sun is said to be 93-million-miles from earth on average, a measurement dating back to Ancient Greece.

Solar Man = 19+15+12+1+18 + 13+1+14 = 93 (O)

God's Son = 7+15+4 + 19 + 19+15+14 = 93 (O) (*son and sun)

Nazareth = 14+1+26+1+18+5+20+8 = 93 (O)

Crucifix = 3+18+21+3+9+6+9+24 = 93 (O)

Also pertinent, the Greek period of time when the distance of the sun was calculated is known as the 'Hellenistic Period', having Reduction Gematria of 93. It meshes well with the 93 Reverse Reduction Gematria of 'Seven Luminaries', what the Greeks called the 7 wandering bodies in the sky, as well as 'Alexander the Great', the most remembered Grecian of all-time. *In Reduction, 'Alexander' also equates to 39.

Hellenistic Period = 8+5+3+3+5+5+9+1+2+9+3 + 7+5+9+9+6+4 = 93 (R)

Seven Luminaries = 8+4+5+4+4 + 6+6+5+9+4+8+9+9+4+8 = 93 (RR)

Alexander the Great = 8+6+4+3+8+4+5+4+9+7+1+4+2+9+4+8+7 = 93 (RR)

Related, the word 'Pagan' in the Ordinal method sums to the number 39, the reflection of the number 93, and corresponding with the number of books in the *Old Testament*. Consider the Pagans use the 'cross' to symbolize the four seasons.

Pagan = 16+1+7+1+14 = 39 (O)

Keep in mind Saturn, associated with time, death and judgment, also shares Gematria of 93, and is the heavenly body worshiped by the Synagogue of Satan, who are the false Jews, who Jesus spoke out against, and which the New Testament warns against. It is entirely possible that the Jews who had Jesus crucified, are from this sect.

Saturn = 19+1+20+21+18+14 = 93 (O)

Even more, Saturn rules Capricorn, the astrological sign from the time of when Jesus's birthday is celebrated. On our Western Astrology charts, Capricorn begins December 21 and concludes on January 19, very fascinating dates, and where the latter can be written 1/19, or 19/1. In Francis Bacon Gematria, where capital letters are taken into 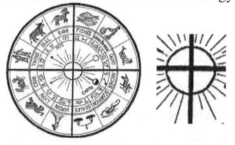 account, 'Saturn' equates to 119, and the date itself, shares a Gematria of 93.

Saturn = 45+1+20+21+18+14 = 119 (Francis Bacon)

January Nineteenth = 8+8+4+6+8+9+2+4+9+4+4+7+4+4+4+7+1 = 93 (RR)

As for the date being written 19/1, that is much like the full name of the Jesuits, which is the 'Society of Jesus'. Keep in mind 191 is the 43rd prime, and the number 43 connects to 'Jesus Christ', just as much as it does to 'killing'; fitting because throughout history, the Jesuits are a known gang of killers, killing in the name of Jesus.

Society of Jesus = 19+15+3+9+5+20+25 +15+6+10+5+19+21+19 = 191 (O)

Jesus = 1+5+1+3+1 = 11; Christ +3+8+9+9+1+2 = 32 (32 paths in Kabbalah)

Jesus Christ = 43 (R)

Killing = 7+9+6+6+9+4+2 = 43 (RR)

Coming back to the number 93, in Sumerian Gematria, Christianity sums to 930, a very similar number to 93, and reminiscent of how Adam, the first man created by God, lives to be exactly 930-years-old.

Christianity = 18+48+108+54+114+120+54+6+84+54+120+150 = 930 (Sumerian)

As we have mentioned, the numbers behind the language come back to the mathematics of this world, and often times to the mathematics regarding 'time'. In that breath, let us now examine the parallel between 'time', 'John', 'Trinity', 'Christian' and 'Solar Deity'. While decoding, let us not forget that time is divided into three phases, the past, present and future. Please also recall that the Tropic of Cancer, and the Tropic of Capricorn, which measure the solstices for the respective northern and southern hemispheres, are separated by 47-degrees. Let us also recall the Freemason logo, with the compasses, set at an angle of exactly 47-degrees.

Time = 20+9+13+5 = 47 (O); *Full Circle = 6+3+3+3+3+9+9+3+3+5 = 47 (R)

John = 10+15+8+14 = 47 (O)

Trinity = 7+9+9+4+9+7+2 = 47 (RR)

Christian = 3+8+9+9+1+2+9+1+5 = 47 (R)

Solar Deity = 1+6+3+1+9+4+5+9+2+7 = 47 (R)

Understanding that the sun and Saturn, as well as the moon, are the bodies in the sky associated with keeping time, I want to include this important Gematria reminder as well.

Bible = 2+9+2+3+5 = 21 (R); *Son = 10+6+5 = 21 (R, S10) (*sun and son)

Saturn = 1+1+2+3+9+5 = 21 (R); Moon = 4+6+6+5 = 21 (R); Lunar = 3+3+5+1+9 = 21 (R)

Recall, Saturn is the 6th planet from the sun, and 21 is the 6th triangular number, meaning if you add 1 through 6 together, it totals 21 (1+2+3+4+5+6 = 21). Also fascinating, is the Ordinal Gematria of 'Bible', and how it corresponds with Reduction Gematria of 'Saturn' when 's' is accounted for as 10, in light of Jesus's ministry beginning at age 30.

Personally, I find this number to be of interest, because after seeking the knowledge that would undo the lies of this world I did not want to live with, such as September 11, an event having much to do with Jesus Christ (in mocking terms), as we'll get to, I was 30-years old when I found Gematria. I had been seeking from the time I was 18, which was my age when 9/11 transpired. It makes me think there is something divine about this number 30, and this age for us as people. Of course, it does break down to the very special digit, number 3, and the root of the 'magic' of number 33. *Also of interest, ages 26 and 28 were hands down the best years of my life, how about you?*

Bible = 2+9+2+12+5 = 30 (O); Saturn = 10+1+2+3+9+5 = 30 (R, S10)

And connecting to 'time' is also the name 'God', the name 'Jesus', the name 'John', the word 'cross', the word 'Christian', the celebration

128

'Christmas', the word 'Church' and also the title 'Solar Deity'. Even the word 'Elohim' in Hebrew (מיקולא) factors in.

God = 7+50+4 = 61 (Jewish Gematria); מיקולא = 13+12+6+19+10+1 = 61 (Hebrew)

Jesus = 17+22+8+6+8 = 61 (RO); John = 17+12+19+13 = 61 (RO)

Cross = 24+9+12+8+8 = 61 (RO); Church = 3+8+21+18+3+8 = 61 (O)

Christian = 6+1+9+9+8+7+9+8+4 = 61 (RR); You = 25+15+21 = 61 (O)

Christmas = 6+1+9+9+8+7+5+8+8 = 61 (RR); Time = 7+18+14+22 = 61 (RO)

Solar Deity = 8+3+6+8+9 + 5+4+9+7+2 = 61 (RR); *Full Circle = 61 (RR)

*Fruit = 21+9+6+18+7 = 61 (RO) (*Recall Fruit of Life from Sacred Geometry*)

Try decoding the hit song, 'Take me to Church'; 61 (R), 74 (RR), 151 (O); 227 (RO)

Don't forget the Flower of Life and its 61-circles. On the date February 22, 2017, you might have heard that in Hollywood, a mysterious statue appeared of Kanye West on the cross, the rapper who in his early career had a hit song *Jesus Walks*. The date that statue appeared, was a date with 61 numerology. Consider February 22 is the 53rd day of the year, and as we learned, the word 'religion' has Gematria of 53 in Reduction (*16th prime*).

2/22/2017 = 2+22+20+17 = 61

On top of that, both 'Hollywood' and 'Kanye West' share Gematria of 33, the age Jesus was supposedly crucified.

Kanye West = 2+1+5+7+5+5+5+1+2 = 33 (R) (*With K11 or S10, Kanye West = 42*)

129

Hollywood = 1+3+6+6+2+4+3+3+5 = 33 (RR) *(With H10, Hollywood = 42)*

Even further, both the artist name and the location connect to the word 'crucifix'. As we decode, do not forget the Tree of Life, especially the darker half, Qliphoth.

Kanye West = 7+8+4+2+4 + 4+4+8+7 = 48 (RR)

Hollywood = 8+6+3+3+7+5+6+6+4 = 48 (R)

Crucifix = 3+9+3+3+9+6+9+6 = 48 (R)

If you take the time to decode more, you'll notice 'Kanye West' in Ordinal sums to 123, and 'crucifix' in Reverse Ordinal also equates to 123. That same year, Kanye West would disappear from media attention until March 15, what is the 74th day of the calendar year, our number connected to Jesus, as well as the number of mentions of the stake and crucifix in the Bible. That date is also the Ides of March, to remember the death of 'Caesar', by 'stabbing', in 44 BCE. In Ordinal Gematria, 'Caesar' sums to 47, and 'stabbing' totals 74. As for the Gematria of 'Ides of March', it sums to 61, like the date numerology of the Kanye West on the cross statue.

Ides of March = 9+5+4+8+3+3+5+8+9+6+1 = 61 (RR)

Consider Kanye West was 39-years-old at the time, the same age Martin Luther King Jr. and Malcolm X were killed by the numbers, as we'll get to in the chapter on the manufactured race war throughout history. Both of those men were assassinated by the "44" code, which is a number representing 'kill' in Ordinal, not unlike the year Caesar died in. For the record, using the Septenary cipher, 'Ides of March' sums to 44 too.

As for Kanye West, a black man being used for this symbol, it is said by many that Jesus was of African descent. In *Revelation 1:14*, about the return of Jesus Christ, it states that Jesus had hair of wool (compare that with the common illustration of long brown hair).

As we read the verse, notice Jesus's hair is said to be white upon the return; this is curious because when Kanye West returned to the media on the 74th day of the year, March 15, 2017, his hair of wool was bleached white. He was also wearing a t-shirt that said 'Cradle of Filth', having Reduction Gematria of 65, just the same as 'Christianity' and 'Knights Templar', the Masonic order that requires its members to be of the faith. If you decode 'Cradle of Filth', notice how it also connects to 'Gospel', 'Tropic of Cancer' and a number of other things related.

Revelation 1:14 King James Version (KJV) His head and his hairs were white like wool, as white as snow; and his eyes were as a flame of fire.

To be fair, I have met one white person in my life that had hair of wool, an Afro that would have made any black person proud. That said I've met a million who didn't, and at the same time, every black person I've ever known, had hair of wool. In light of this, I want to show you what is fascinating about the Septenary Gematria of 'Jesus Christ'.

Jesus Christ = 4+5+6+6+6+3+6+5+5+6+7 = 59 (Septenary)

As you will learn in the race war chapter, this is a number that has been stamped on black people throughout history, and it is the reason Motown records opened its doors in 1959 and the reason 'Black History Month' ends on the 59th day of the year. Let us take a moment to decode some words that should make the coding of this number on black history abundantly clear. As you will learn, a number of famous black people have been murdered in relation to this number as well, which we'll get to.

Negro = 14+5+7+18+15 = 59 (O); Slave = 19+12+1+22+5 = 59 (O)

Blues = 2+12+21+5+19 = 59 (O); Rasta = 18+1+19+20+1 = 59 (O)

Jigaboo = 10+9+7+1+2+15+15 = 59 (O)

Tiger = 20+9+7+5+18 = 59 (O) (Think about Eeny, meeny, miny, moe…)

Woods = 4+12+12+23+8 = 59 (RO)

*Kill = 10+9+20+20 = 59 (Jewish Gematria)

Often times when I teach about this subject online, the race of Jesus, and the coding of the number on a race of people, some take offense. Please know that I do not aim to offend, I only mean to shed light on information most people are completely oblivious to. I also mean to bring logic; consider what portion of the world the *Bible* is set in and the story of Jesus Christ, it is not historically a place white people are from. For one more relevant point on the matter, consider that the Kanye West statue appeared in February, what is 'Black History Month'. This title has Gematria of 93, like 'crucifix'.

Black History Month = 7+6+8+6+7+1+9+8+7+3+9+2+5+3+4+7+1 = 93 (RR)

Martin Luther King Jr. = 4+1+9+2+9+5+3+3+2+8+5+9+2+9+5+7 + 1+9 = 93 (R)

Malcolm X = 13+1+12+3+15+12+13+24 = 93 (O)

Rosa   Louise   McCauley   Parks   = 9+6+1+1+3+6+3+9+1+5+4+3+3+1+3+3+5+7+7+1+9+2+1 = 93 (R)

For a little more, think about the town of Tuskegee, where Rosa Parks was born, and a town that has a lot to do with black American history.

Tuskegee = 20+21+19+11+5+7+5+5 = 93 (O)

Again, Malcolm X and Martin Luther King Jr. were both killed at 39 (same age Kanye was when the statue appeared), and we'll learn a lot more about their deaths and more ahead. As a reminder, reflections of numbers are equals, thus 39 is 93. For now, just to help make a point, we'll look at the date Rosa Parks died, October 24, 2005.

10/24/2005 = 10+24+20+05 = 59 (Negro, Ordinal) (Kill, Jewish Gematria)

10/24/05 = 10+24+05 = 39 (Reflection of 93)

Before concluding our discussion on Jesus Christ, Christianity and the Greeks, there are a few more things I want to show about the *Gospels*, the first 4-books of the *New Testament,* where the story of Jesus Christ is contained. From these same books, the most remembered verse when it comes to Jesus Christ, is *John 3:16.* The verse follows.

John 3:16 New International Version (NIV) For God so loved the world that he gave his one and only Son, that whoever believes in him shall not perish but have eternal life.

For starters, in Hebrew Gematria, Jesus Christ (ושי) sums to 316, not unlike the verse number, *3:16.* The Hebrew Gematria is as follows.

ושי = 10 + 300 + 6 = 316 (Hebrew Gematria)

Second, in Reduction Gematria, the verse equates to 499, what is the 95th prime number. This is fascinating because 'December twenty-fifth' sums to 95, and it the Society of Jesus's birthday, September 27, that leaves 95-days left in the year. Even more, if you write out 'six hundred sixty six', it totals 95 in Reduction, and you'll recall, 'Jesus Christ', in Ordinal Gematria, sums to 151, what is the 36th prime number, where 666 is the 36th triangular number, the number of a man.

From my own life I have a story about the number 151. I was visiting the town of Yakima, Washington for the first time in my life, Friday, October 13, 2017, and while in town I stopped by the local gas station to put some fuel in the tank. While I was waiting in line to pay for the gasoline, a man with a cane was standing directly before me, and noticeably shaking. I was ready to catch him in case he fell. When it was his turn to talk to the attendant, he asked if he could use his EBT Card to purchase some hot food; if you don't know, that is a welfare payment card. The attendant responded, "NO, WE DON'T ACCEPT THAT!" in a noticeably forceful way. To me it felt cruel, and I wondered if there was some racial animosity behind it, because the man with the cane was dark as night and the attendant was not. After being told no, the man began to move out of line but I asked him to wait, and I gave him one of the two $10-bills I was holding in my hand that I had intended to use for gasoline. When he reached for the bill, the grip of his hand surprised me; it was very strong. A little harder and I might not be able to type about it. While he held my hand and the bill, he smiled, and he said, "God bless you." Then he turned to the cashier and said, "Jesus is always looking out!" I happened to check the time at the same moment because I needed to be somewhere soon. Just as he had made his remark about Jesus, the time was precisely 1:51 in the afternoon. After that he ordered the hot food he desired and I told him to keep the change so he could get another meal if he was hungry later. He thanked me again and I told him it was my pleasure. After that I went in my car and cried. I felt guilty because I had lost much of my faith for seemingly so long, but in that moment it was restored, even though my gas tank was not. At the end of this book, I'll tell you more about this same story, and more. But I assure you truth seeker, being aware of this knowledge, you'll see the magic of these numbers in real time, and again, I do truly believe there is a very divine element at play when it comes to this mathematical language. That is something I have no doubt about.

Back on the subject of *John 3:16*, the same verse when decoded in Ordinal Gematria, equates to 1201. In this study, 1201 is the exact same as 121, because the zeros are of no value. As you'll recall, 121 is the 11th prime number, and in Reduction Gematria, 'Jesus' sums to 11. As we also learned earlier, when you add 1 through 11 together, it totals 66, making 66 the 11th triangular number. It is the 66th book of most Bibles that is about the return of Jesus Christ, *'Revelation'*, which also has an Ordinal value of 121. So how fitting it is, that these numbers are found in this well remembered verse, that you'll often see proud Christians sporting around town on their clothing.

134

Let us now conclude our elementary learning of the encoding of the *Bible* with some final points concerning the length of the *Old Testament, Gospels* and *New Testament*. Beginning with the *Old Testament*, the entire 39-books are 929-chapters long. This is a fascinating number, the 158th prime number. In Reverse Ordinal Gematria, 'Freemasonry', which is very much based in the *Old Testament*, equates to 158. Also intriguing, is that on the Gregorian calendar, September 29, a date we'll learn more about later, is the day leaving 93-days left in the year. In Jewish Gematria, 'United States of America' also sums to 929. We'll learn more about the relevance of both of these stats in the chapters ahead on Freemasonry and the U.S.A. For the record, '*Old Testament*' in Reduction sums to 40, same as 'United States', and in Ordinal, 'U.S.' sums to 40 just as well. Some say Jesus was crucified at age 40, and not age 33. For the record, 'crucify' does sum to 40 in Reduction Gematria.

As for the *New Testament*, it is 260-chapters, not too far off from 26, as we learned, matching the word 'religion' in English Extended Gematria. If you add the total number of chapters from the *Old Testament* and *New Testament,* it sums to 1189. As we learned, the number 89 is a Fibonacci number, and it happens to be the 11th Fibonacci number in the sequence. Knowing that, think about 1189-chapters in light of the Fibonacci numbers being connected to God, and the *Bible* being made in tribute to God. Even more, the *New Testament* begins with the *Gospels* that are 89-chapters long. Beyond the Fibonacci sequence, the word 'Number' sums to 89 in Reverse Ordinal, the name 'Greek' does as well, the word 'religion' sums to 89 in Ordinal, and so does the name 'King James', who of course has a *Bible* named in his honor, that released his year of turning 45-years.

Number = 13+6+14+25+22+9 = 89 (RO); Greek = 20+9+22+22+16 = 89 (RO)

Religion = 18+5+12+9+7+9+15+14 = 89 (O)

King James = 11+9+14+7+10+1+13+5+19 = 89 (O)

As you should be able to gather, nothing is arbitrary about the *Bible* when it comes to the numbers that are transparent, or the ones that are encoded. Ahead when we learn about King James and his *KJV*, I'm going to reveal something very fascinating to you about the number of the beast that we have not yet uncovered. As a reminder truth seeker, there is always more, and now that you know the code, you can discover what more there is. I've taught you how to fish if you will. Speaking of which, you might want to try the Gematria of 'fisherman'. Before moving on, let's briefly discuss some of the Greek greats, and consider how their legacy has impacted the holy text, as we know it.

It is Pythagoras (570–495 BCE), the Greek philosopher, thought to be divine, considered by many to be the first mathematician in history, credited with creating the musical scale, who is said to have been the person who introduced Isopsephy to his native Greece, only after studying Gematria in Egypt under Jewish and Hermetic scholars, centuries before the birth of Iēsous (Jesus). His purpose as a man was advancing understanding of science and spirituality with the goal of attaining a philosophical based society through knowledge, as opposed to a material and possession oriented one, not unlike Jesus. The mottos of his school were "All is number" and "God is number". Without Pythagoras, the *Bible* as we know it, probably would not be.

One of Pythagoras's most important pupils, a Pythagorean, was Philolaus (470-385 BCE) whose writings document the achievements of his teacher, including his lessons on Isopsephy and Gematria. In fact, the only way historians know of Pythagoras is through the writings of Philolaus. He is also a student credited with helping discover that earth is not the center of the universe by using mathematical proofs derived from studying at Pythagoras's school, an understanding still with us today. After the time of Pythagoras and Philolaus, the Pythagorean tradition carried on in Platonism, an evolved study, including the work of Pythagoras, Philolaus and Plato (427-347 BCE), that arose 600 years after Plato's passing, with the philosopher Plotinus (204-270 CE), who had his teachings made into writings known as the *Enneads,* summing to 26 in Reduction (matching the Reverse Reduction of Greek), by Porphyry (234-305 CE), his greatest scholar. The works teach a philosophy based on three principles; the One, the Intellect and the Soul, not far off from the Father, the Son and the Holy Spirit, what is the 'Trinity', which are both three in number, not unlike the angles of a triangle, a sacred shape to Geometry, symbolizing strength and measure. In light of this being part of Pythagoras' legacy, let us not forget the Pythagorean theorem, $a^2 + b^2 = c^2$, as studied in Geometry class worldwide. To make sure the point is understood, it is these historical figures and these philosophical and spiritual teachings over the years, with mathematical basis, that have influenced the Abrahamic Religions, Judaism, Christianity and Islam, also three in number, as well as the occult. As we are coming to understand, historically, the ideas of science, mathematics and spirituality were all part of one greater study that was about understanding our place in this world and how to perfect our way of living. In this belief system, God is seen as the all-perfect creator, and in this world of beliefs, nothing known is more perfect than the number. As we learned earlier, the word 'perfect' and 'number' also share Ordinal Gematria of 73, a number composed of the digits symbolizing divine completion (7), and light (3), respectively. On the subject, Catholic Bibles are 73-books in length, and 73 is the 21st prime number, bringing us back to the Gematria of '*Bible*', '*Jesuit*' and more.

For another important Grecian, Plutarch (46-120 CE), the Greek biographer and author, he once wrote, "Plato said God geometrizes continually", meaning God's mysterious work is mathematically oriented. Once upon a time, I might have balked at such a thought, but no longer truth seeker. Having been living with knowledge of the code for the last 4-years of my life, I think it is safe to say God is the master mathematician, and God's geometrizing can be observed in many places throughout the world including our own lives, something I have only briefly began to share about, and something you will begin to recognize now knowing what you are learning at this very moment. The more you learn, the more apparent this mysterious reality will become. If you have never listened to my weekly radio program on *Truth Frequency Radio,* the *Gematria Effect,* each and every week people call in to share their own mysterious observations, and I hope that one day soon I hear your tales as well.

For another once active Greek practitioner and celebrator of Geometry, Phidias (480-430 BCE), the Greek sculptor, whose accomplishments were documented by Plato, including one the Seven Wonders of the Ancient World, the statue of Zeus at Olympia, is known for using the mathematics of the Golden Ratio, Phi, 1.61, in all of his works because of its mathematical significance and its aesthetics to the human eye. As we covered to begin the chapter, 'aesthetics' sums to 161 in the language of Gematria, not far off from 1.61. Because of Phidias's commitment to Phi, the 21st letter

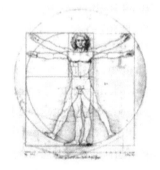

of the Greek alphabet, Phi, is titled in his honor, taking the first 3-letters of his name. As we documented earlier, 21 is the 8th Fibonacci number, and it also has the prime relationship with 73, symbolizing perfection. Consider further, the number 8 symbolizes the infinite, or the eternally existent as Pythagoras once put it, and again, Phi, 1.61, is considered to be the "fingerprint of God", omnipresent, omnipotent and everlasting.

If you were paying attention, the 7-Greeks and their lasting impact on history we just acknowledged- Pythagoras, Plato, Philolaus, Plotinus, Porphyry, Plutarch, and Phidias, each have names beginning with P, the 16th letter in the English alphabet; a number made of the same numerical digits as Phi (1.61), 1 and 6, and as mentioned prior, in Greek, the 16th letter is Pi, or π. Even more, showing the clear relationship with our English alphabet, when you write out Pi, using Reduction Gematria, it sums to 16.

Pi = 7+9 = 16 (R)

Better yet, the number 'sixteen' when written out as a word also has a direct parallel to the Gematria of 'Phi', as follows.

Sixteen = 1+9+6+2+5+5+5 = 33 (R); Phi = 16+8+9 = 33 (O)

Regarding Phi being the "fingerprint of God", in Hebrew Reduction, 'Elohim' equates to 16 as well. The math is as follows.

מיקולא = 1+3+6+1+1+4 = 16 (Hebrew Reduction)

Again, it is Phi that is aesthetically pleasing to the human eye, and has been used in artwork since the time of the Greeks for this exact reason. Let me show you one more important encoding of this word, 'aesthetic', while keeping in mind that Phi is said to be the "fingerprint of God". Through this example, we will connect the encoding with a very special number to the '*Holy Bible*', from the story of the '*Miraculous Catch*', where Jesus performs a miracle, helping his followers catch a plentiful amount of fish, 153.

John 21:10-11 New International Version (NIV)

10 Jesus said to them, "Bring some of the fish you have just caught." 11 So Simon Peter climbed back into the boat and dragged the net ashore. It was full of large fish, 153, but even with so many the net was not torn.

Aesthetic = 26+22+8+7+19+22+7+18+24 = 153 (RO)

Holy Bible = 19+12+15+2 + 25+18+25+15+22 = 153 (RO)

The Bible = 7+19+22 + 25+18+25+15+22 = 153 (RO)

This number relates to God. The number 153 is the 17th triangular number. Also, the number 351 is the 26th triangular number. Both numbers 17 and 26 are in relation.

God = 7+6+4 = 17 (R); God = 7+15+4 = 26 (O)

On the subject of numbers 17 and 153, using Reduction Gematria, the name *'Miraculous Catch'* sums to 59, what is the 17th prime number, and as we learned, a number having parallels to Jesus Christ through the Septenary cipher. For a few more observations on the word 'aesthetic', let us use our complimentary ciphers we learned in Chapter 4. Keep in mind that the word has to do with beauty and a set of underlying rules, or guiding principles, both of which the Holy Bible is most certainly constructed with.

Aesthetic = 1+5+6+7+6+5+7+5+3 = 45 (Septenary)

Holy Bible = 8+6+3+7 + 2+9+2+3+5 = 45 (R)

Holy Bible = 1+3+6+2 + 7+9+7+6+4 = 45 (RR)

Aesthetic = 36+40+54+55+43+40+55+44+38 = 405 (Satanic)

Holy Bible = 43+50+47+60 + 37+44+37+47+40 = 405 (Satanic)

From the first verse of the *Holy Bible*, until the last verse, the code is intact. To close, let me reveal something about Genesis 1:1 that we have not yet uncovered, bringing us back to what we first learned about the Geometry of the English language in Chapter 2.

Genesis 1 New International Version (NIV) In the beginning God created the heavens and the earth.

In the beginning God created the heavens and the earth = 9+4+7+1+4+7+4+2+9+4+4+9+4+2+2+3+5+6+9+4+8+7+4+5+7+1+4+1 +4+8+5+4+4+8 +8+4+5+7+1+4+4+8+9+7+1 = **227** (RR) (*Earth = **227** in Satanic Gematria)

Recall that when you write out 'Three-hundred-sixty', the degrees of a circle, it sums to 227 in Ordinal Gematria, and when you write out 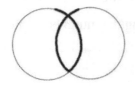 'Twenty-two divided by seven' it equates to 314, very much like Pi, 3.14. Consider the earth is circling in perfect orbit. Also as a reminder, if you're on a PC, and you type alt+227, you will generate the symbol for Pi (π) on your screen in your word processing program. Going back to our chapter on Sacred Geometry, we learned that the belief is God created the world by replicating the circle 7-times, what is known as the Seed of Life. That said, let us now decode the opening verse of the *Bible*, from the *KJV*. The KJV changes the word 'heavens' to the singular, 'heaven'. There are two reasons for this.

Genesis 1 King James Version (KJV) In the beginning God created the heaven and the earth.

In the beginning God created the heaven and the earth = 18+13+7+19+22+25+22+20+18+13+13+18+13+20 + 20+12+23+24+9+22+26+7+22+23+7+19+22+19+22+26+5+22+13+26+ 13+23+7+19+2 2 + 22+26+9+7+19 = **777** (RO) (777? 7-days of creation)

In the beginning God created the heaven and the earth = 9+5+2+8+5+2+5+7+9+5+5+9+5+7+7+6+4+3+9+5+1+2+5+4+2+8+5+8 +5+1+4+5+5+1 +5+4+2+8+5+5+1+9+2+8 = **222** (R)

As above, so below = 26+8+26+25+12+5+22+8+12+25+22+15+12+4 = **222** (RO)

　　*God created the above, and the below　　*Number 2 symbolizes duality

TEN

CHAPTER

◄∞►

Who are 'THEY'? Freemasonry & Rosicrucian Order

You hear it often, *"they"*. There's even a movie made about them, *They Live,* where 'they' are destroyed when the protagonist takes down the media. The word comes up time and time again when people are talking about conspiracy related matters, something that is commonly wrongfully called "conspiracy theory", when the things being discussed are truly <u>conspiracy fact</u>. So many people who have conspiracy related conversations see the wrongdoing in the world, and the scapegoats blamed for the wrongdoing, such as men in caves, anorexic teens packing more heat than Rambo, MIT brothers with backpacks posing on the cover of *Rolling Stone*, and disgruntled $100-per-hand-poker players in Las Vegas, just to name a few; but they aren't certain who is pulling the strings and creating the mass confusion and chaos, because the responsible parties are something like the man behind the curtain in *The Wizard of Oz,* operating out of sight of the general public. This leads to many people accusing the wrongdoers of being the entity known as 'they'. That is about to change however, because who 'they' are is very clear, once you know the code. And for the record, a "conspiracy theory" is deemed to be something that has no factual or evidence basis, thus what you are reading in this book could never be considered as such, since everything within is evidence based and well supported, and only going to become more and more supported with each passing page.

Let us begin identifying who 'they' are and what 'they' are about with the term "conspiracy theory", a derogatory term to dismiss the truth seeker and speaker, that is the creation of 'they'. It was a term coined by Richard Hofstadter, a public intellectual, historian, and professor at Columbia University, and a term pushed by the CIA (see CIA Document 1035-960, released in 1976 with the Freedom of Information Act (FOIA)), after the very numerological assassination of 'Kennedy', November 22, 1963, which happened in the middle of Dealey Plaza, named after a $33^{rd\,\circ}$ Scottish Rite Freemason, not unlike Abraham Zapruder, who was also of the $33^{rd\,\circ}$ and is remembered for making the assassination film of the 35th President, from that very memorable date, 11/22. For a little Gematria practice, why don't you take a moment to decode 'Kennedy' with the Reduction method to see how nicely it goes with the collection of number 33s hidden in plain sight? And in light of JFK being the 35th President, the lone 'Catholic' President to date, decode the name of the religion with the same Reduction method as well to see how they jive. If you want to take it a step further, decode the name of the same 'religion' with the Reverse Reduction method, and notice how it corresponds with his age of death, 46-years, and the number of books in the *Old Testament* of the *Catholic Bible*, which is 46 in count. Of course with Gematria being a biblical code, from the *Torah,* it is important to note *Genesis 46* begins with a 'sacrifice', a word having Reduction Gematria of 46, and in Hebrew, both 'murder' and 'kill' equate to number 46 as well. When you decode 'Kennedy' and 'Catholic', you won't be disappointed, but you will be

144

collecting some mounting evidence of who 'they' are, and how 'they' operate, a pile you'll soon need a secretary to help keep in order.

Before I prove to you that 'Freemasonry' in high places, including the U.S. Federal Government and Catholic Church is who 'they' are, and who 'they' have been since before the United States even existed, I want to show you what happened to this man, Richard Hofstadter, used by the CIA to push the term, "conspiracy theory", a term that has had a profoundly negative impact on all those who quest for truth. All my good people who speak truth know how it is from the sleeping masses (or what I call the American Dreamers here in the States). When you speak truth to the zombie-like masses, you'll hear it nine times out of ten. *"What are you, some kind of conspiracy theorist?"* When I was 18, I used to explain to people that it didn't make sense 'they' could not recover the plane parts, or bodies from the wreckage sites of September 11, 2001, but somehow 'they' reported recovering "terrorist passports", "box-cutter knives", and even "turbans". Those logical points would be greeted with the same programmed-responses, ranging from, "conspiracy theorist", to "mom's basement", to "tinfoil hat", and right on down the line, by almost everyone. I told my family and friends who would listen then, *"I think the people of this land are under some sort of magical spell, not unlike a tale from a Disney film."* At the same time I'd tell those who gave the brain -dead robotic replies to my logical and truthful points, *"No, and are you some kind of coincidence theorist?"* In the near future I intend to put out a t-shirt with the **"coincidence theorist"** slogan so you can hand them out to these people when they cross your path. I'm telling you now I'm going to have to print A LOT!

As for Richard Hofstadter, the man who coined the divisive and played-out term "conspiracy theory", he died October 24, 1970, a date with the right kind of numerology for being remembered for tarnishing the truth about 'conspiracy', and for being used as a 'CIA' asset. He also died 79-days after his August 6 birthday, a distance in days corresponding with the Ordinal Gematria of the word 'murder', something you'll learn a lot more about in the chapter on murder by numbers. The number 79 also connects to the label 'conspiracist', what is a person who supports "conspiracy theory". Even better, he died at age 54, relatively young, and a number perfectly corresponding with the initials 'JFK', as well as the Gematria of 'Dealey Plaza' and 'Jesuit Order', the latter of which are the Masonic killers within the Catholic Church, known by historians to be connected to the assassination of Abraham Lincoln and more. Again, Hofstadter's 'conspiracy theory' term was derived in connection to the people who were questioning the government's Warren Commission findings and the media's reporting on the death of JFK, from the infamous day in history. Let us now examine the date numerology for October 24, 1970, which breaks down to both '123' and '51', because those two numbers point directly to the Gematria of 'conspiracy'.

$$10/24/1970 = 10+24+19+70 = 123; \quad 10/24/1970 = 10+24+(1+9+7+0) = 51$$

In Ordinal Gematria, 'conspiracy' sums to 123, not unlike the breakdown of 'ABC', which is how simple this code is, that 'they' operate by. *Can I get a little Jackson 5? And yes, Michael was reported dead by the code.* Also, in Reduction Gematria, 'conspiracy' sums to 51, same as 'Freemason' when 's' is made to be 10, and same as 'Federal' in Ordinal Gematria. Think about Area-51, the federal government territory specifically associated with 'conspiracy', in the 47th state. Even better, the common stereotype, 'tinfoil-hat', shares 51 Gematria just the same. And for an even bigger laugh, Reynolds Wrap aluminum foil was released as a new consumer product in 1947, the same year as the 'UFO' landing in New Mexico, the 47th state. *And yes, UFO news in the mainstream has always been the work of 'they', reported by the numbers.*

As we progress, you'll see just how many connections there are between the Freemasons and the various terminology pertaining to conspiracy through the language of Gematria, a largely Masonic language. This is no coincidence. The Masonic network at the top controls this world with conspiracy, and that is exactly why 'they' have programmed the masses to balk at the word, so as not to even consider the truth. In case you are not certain of what a conspiracy is, it is a **secret plan** to do something harmful, or unlawful. Think about that within the context of Freemasonry, a secret society…

Conspiracy = 3+15+14+19+16+9+18+1+3+25 = 123 (O)

Conspiracy = 3+6+5+1+7+9+9+1+3+7 = 51 (R)

Tinfoil-Hat = 2+9+5+6+6+9+3+8+1+2 = 51 (R)

Freemason = 6+9+5+5+4+1+10+6+5 = 51 (R, S10)

Federal = 6+5+4+5+18+1+12 = 51 (O)

Let us not forget that Washington D.C., the headquarters of the federal government, is also the headquarters of the Scottish Rite of Freemasonry. Very quickly, notice the overlap with 'Scottish Rite', 'conspiracy' and 'coincidence'.

Scottish Rite = 1+3+6+2+2+9+1+8+9+9+2+5 = 57 (R)

Conspiracy = 6+3+4+8+2+9+9+8+6+2 = 57 (RR)

Coincidence = 3+6+9+5+3+9+4+5+5+3+5 = 57 (R)

Tinfoil Hat = 7+9+4+3+3+9+6+1+8+7 = 57 (RR)

As we advance through the remaining chapters, I will enlighten you to what "coincidence theory" programming is. With every major propaganda event contrived in the media, a number of "coincidences" to go with are contrived for the gullible audience. In recent years, a clear example of these tactics was the story of the 'Mormon' missionary, Mason Wells, who reportedly survived the April 15, 2013 Boston Marathon Bombing hoax, the Friday November 13, 2015 Paris terror attack false flag, and the March 22, 2016 Brussels, Belgium bombing hoax. If you are not familiar with this story, please look it up, and please don't overlook the name 'Mason'. If you decode 'Friday the

Thirteenth', you'll also notice it sums to 223 in Ordinal Gematria, not unlike the March 22, 22/3 date of the Belgium attack. Again, 'Masonic' in Jewish Gematria equates to 223, and 'The Synagogue of Satan' sums to the same number in Ordinal.

Masonic = 13+1+19+15+14+9+3 = 74 (O)

Mormon = 14+12+9+14+12+13 = 74 (RO) (Mormon Church is based in Freemasonry)

Mason Wells = 5+8+8+3+4+4+22+6+6+8 = 74 (RR, E22)

In the next chapter you'll learn how 'George Washington' himself was murdered by the code, not uncommon, even for members of the fraternity. Consider 'George Washington' in Reverse Reduction sums to 74, just the same as 'Masonic' and 'killing' in Ordinal Gematria. And at the same time, as mentioned, the word 'murder' sums to 79 in Ordinal Gematria, and 'conspiracist' totals 79 in Reverse Reduction Gematria, matching the amount of days after Richard Hofstadter's birthday to his death. As you'll discover, all celebrities who have bitten the dust prematurely have done so by this code, and it has always been synced with their respective birthdays, from overdoses to plane crashes. Even more, the date of Richard's passing also had a numerology connection to 34, which corresponds with 'murder' just the same, using the Reduction cipher.

Murder = 13+21+18+4+5+18 = 79 (O)

Conspiracist = 6+3+4+8+2+9+9+8+6+9+8+7 = 79 (RR)

Murder = 4+3+9+4+5+9 = 34 (R); *10/24 = 10+24 = 34

Richard's day of passing, October 24, also happens to be the day that leaves 68-days left in the year, not unlike his August 6 birthday, which can be expressed 6/8. Of course, in Gematria, 'CIA' sums to 68. Speaking of which, in the year '68, MLK and RFK (JFK's brother) would be killed by the numbers, among others. That was also the year 9-1-1 was made the national emergency dialing code, World Trade

Center construction began, and 'George W. Bush' would graduate from Yale's Skull and Bones, 33-years before 2001. Adding insult to injury, Bush's July 6 birthday, the 187th day of the year, is a span of 68-days from September 11. Don't forget his father was the head of the CIA before becoming the Vice President and then President. Ahead you'll also learn how 'Yale' sums to 43 in Ordinal, and how Bush II was the 43rd President, pairing nicely with his brother being the 43rd Governor of Florida (remember the Florida recount that changed the outcome of the 2000 election from Gore winning to 'Bush'?), and his father being the 43rd Vice President before becoming President Bush I (or was it King George I?). Not by chance, 'Masonic' also shares the Gematria of 43 in Reverse Reduction, but now we're getting ahead of ourselves! Before we spoil too many goodies for chapters ahead, let's decode 'CIA'. And while we're at it, let's decode 'Mom's Basement' too, since I'm pretty sure the CIA made this phrase stick with the mass-media they largely own and operate, paid for with our tax dollars. *Personally, despite never having lived in a home with a basement, or with my mother since days after turning 18-years-old, I have been told at least 1,000 times and counting to get out of my mom's basement, especially when I have shared truth online.*

CIA = 24+18+26 = 68 (RO)

Mom's Basement = 5+3+5+8+7+8+8+4+5+4+4+7 = 68 (RR)

As for Richard Hofstadter passing at age 54, the Gematria of 'JFK', 'Dealey Plaza', and 'Jesuit Order' are as follows.

JFK   =   17+21+16   =   54   (RO);   Freemasonic   = 6+9+5+5+4+1+1+6+5+9+3 = 54 (R)

Dealey Plaza = 5+4+8+6+4+2+2+6+8+1+8 = 54 (RR)

Jesuit Order = 1+5+1+3+9+2+6+9+4+5+9 = 54 (R)

Mr. Hofstadter's cause of death was reported as 'cancer', which is a common cause of death for people murdered by the numbers. Who would think twice about it in a world where thousands perish this way daily? In terms of conspiracy, the way we are fed, which is the predominant reason for the rampant rates of cancer in the United States and elsewhere, is one of the largest conspiracies of all, and that shouldn't be any secret to anyone seeing as how the U.S. federal government and its "elected" officials actively work to make sure we the people cannot even know what is in our food by passing legislation in congress to achieve this information blackout. Think about it. This is a fact that most people are either oblivious to, or shrug their shoulders at. Your elected officials, who you pay for, are working to make sure you cannot know what is in your food. Something tells me if we could find out what they're hiding, one of the ingredients we're not being told about is, "brain-dead retarded poisoning". And please don't start crying that you don't like the word retarded. The word means stunted, and if you're not an *American Dreamer*, you should notice the people around you couldn't be anymore intellectually stunted than they are. As they say, you are what you eat. Now, very quickly, let me show you something about the words 'cancer', 'chemo', and 'kill'; it's all part of the buildup to the proof of who 'they' are and what 'they' are about. Before decoding, you should know that you don't cure your body with chemo radiation, which only kills more cells; you cure it with eating right. If you're not up on nutrition, you're in luck, because I am. The human body is designed to eat a plant-based diet, which is why we have the intestines and teeth of an herbivore. Remember this, *just because you can, doesn't mean you should.* And yes, I am talking about meat and dairy consumption because animal protein kills slowly by clogging arteries and causing cancerous mutations within the body, what is documented scientific fact. Take a look at your fellow

Americans, how many of them are obese with guts sticking out like a stuffed pillow?

How many people are needlessly keeling over from heart attacks? How many people have cholesterol rates twice the normal level? These are the clearly unhealthy results of eating an animal-based diet, with

God knows what injected into them (steroids, hormones, preservatives, and worse), our bodies are not designed to metabolize efficiently, or properly. In the wild, animals that eat meat can eat it raw, and they have short, direct, intestinal tracts; unlike ours, which are long, and anything but straight.

Think about what happens to you if you try to eat raw meat. It is definite illness, potentially death. This is why 'Susan G. Komen' loves to advertise with their pink 'ribbon' on the products that give you cancer, such as beef and eggs, it is mockery.

"Keep eating what kills you, and send us some more shekels so we can keep searching for the cure that was found a century ago, muhahahahaha!" The cure is a plant-based diet.

Kill = 11+9+12+12 = 44 (O); Genocide = 7+5+5+6+3+9+4+5 = 44 (R)

Cancer = 3+1+14+3+5+18 = 44 (O); Chemo = 3+8+5+13+15 = 44 (O)

*JFK was the 35th President, but he was also the **44th term** President.

Speaking of 'they', just wait until we decode the name of the cancer charity fraud 'Susan G. Komen', the name of a woman who was supposedly diagnosed with breast cancer at age 33 (and probably never even existed), an age matching the Reduction Gematria of 'ribbon'. You'll find that her name in particular has Gematriot overlap with 'Freemasonry' in 3 out of the 4 base ciphers, plus connects to 'kill', just like 'cancer', and more. That shouldn't surprise considering the capital-G right in the middle. For kicks, and because it relates, let's take a moment to decode the name of the false charity, which is only meant to steal money from the ignorant and gullible public. The name of the charity is 'Susan G. Komen for the Cure'. While we're at it, we ought to decode 'cure' as well, as it sums to 47, a number you have learned a thing or two about already.

151

Susan   G.   Komen   for   the   Cure   =
1+3+1+1+5+7+2+6+4+5+5+6+6+9+2+8+5 +3+3+9+5 = 96 (R)

Freemason = 6+18+5+5+13+1+19+15+14 = 96 (O)

Cure = 3+21+18+5 = 47 (O) (47-degrees on Freemason logo)

Now you know why the 'cure' never comes, despite the rapid advancement of technology in computers, automobiles, pills that make the 'phallus' pop, and even cosmetic things, such as breast and butt cheek implants. It is profit over people, and cancer is big business, as you well know. More importantly, when people donate money to this false charity, it goes to 'they', which means anywhere but cancer research. In all likelihood, it is probably being used to fund the next cancer causing thing our congress will keep us from knowing is in our food. The next time you see the pink 'ribbon', say no.

For a bit more on conspiracy, before we get to the proof of who 'they' are, in 2016, Progressive Insurance and Pizza Hut released ads making fun of "conspiracy theorists", targeting those who seek truth, including 9/11 and more. With regards to Pizza Hut, the company was opened in '58, and turned 58-years-old in 2016, just in time for their commercial, that was made by 'they'. In 2017, FedEx followed in their footsteps, releasing an ad making fun of 9/11-truthers with a commercial about a conspiracy related bookstore called 'Conspiracy Books', and in the background of the ad, showcasing a giant THEY poster, with the word in caps. Next to THEY, it was followed with the words, "control all". Notice the following Gematria, and pay mind to the fact that the JFK assassination happened in '63. By the way, 2016 is the 63rd triangular number, and the first of these commercials released in the respective year, 2016.

Conspiracy Books = 3+6+5+1+7+9+9+1+3+7+2+6+6+2+1 = 68 (R)

THEY Control All = 7+6+5+2+3+2+1+7+5+2+2+1+2+2 = 47 (Septenary)

THEY Control All = 2+8+5+7 + 3+6+5+2+9+6+3 + 1+3+3 = 63 (R)

Don't overlook the fact that the 2017 release of the 'commercial' was 54-years after 1963. The same FedEx ad, which we'll talk more about in the 9/11 chapter, and same with the Pizza Hut ad, ends with the bookstore employee saying to the FedEx worker, "If your name is even Bill", to which he replies, "Actually, it's William."

Bill = 20+23+2+2 = 47 (ALW Kabbalah)

William = 4+9+6+6+9+8+5 = 47 (RR)

Commercial = 3+6+4+4+5+9+3+9+1+3 = 47 (RR)

*The commercial is supposed to be set in Seattle, on the 47th Parallel North

*The Seattle's Space Needle has a rotating restaurant that does a 360° turn every 47-minutes

If you haven't seen these ads, they're a web search away and it should lead you to boycott these companies that participate in this type of deception and mockery. In the case of the Progressive ad, it features two older men, in their mother's basement, listening to recordings in reverse, and the phrase the commercial repeats is "lively little locksmith, lively little locksmith". Let me show you why they chose this phrase. Keep in mind we just learned 'conspiracy' has Ordinal Gematria of 123.

Lively little locksmith =
6+9+5+4+6+2+6+9+7+7+6+4+6+3+6+7+8+5+9+7+1 = 123 (RR)

In Reduction Gematria, the same phrase also equates to 'conspiracy theorist' as well as 'mother's basement'. The math is as follows.

Lively little locksmith =
3+9+4+5+3+7+3+9+2+2+3+5+3+6+3+2+1+4+9+2+8 = 93 (R)

Mother's Basement = 5+3+7+10+4+9+8+7+8+8+4+5+4+4+7 = 93 (RR)

Conspiracy   Theorist   =   3+6+5+1+7+9+9+1+3+7   + 2+8+5+6+9+9+1+2 = 93 (R)

In the Progressive commercial where they're listening to recordings in reverse, a stereotypical "conspiracy theorist" activity, the purpose of the ad is to degrade conspiracy researchers as idiotic 'propaganda' pushers who need to grow up, and get out of their 'mom's basement'. The reason 'they' really want the truth seekers to move on from the truth, is because they're afraid of being exposed, and more people waking up to their lies and their agenda. It's just like what it says in the *Talmud*, if the people ever find out the truth, those who abide by the *Talmud* are dead meat, and it is the same *Talmud* thumpers, who call us goyim, who think we're too dumb for our own good, that make these ads.

Propaganda = 16+18+15+16+1+7+1+14+4+1 = 93 (O)

Recording = 18+5+3+15+18+4+9+14+7 = 93 (O)

For one last point about the Progressive commercial, when the mother calls on her son who appears to be in his mid-40s, if not older, hunching over, with thick rimmed glasses, and staring into his computer, his name is 'Tom', not too far off from the Progressive Insurance character 'Flo', who appears in the ad as well. In REVERSE Reduction Gematria, 'Tom' sums to 33, same as Flo, forwards. Again, a big part of the ad is listening to things in reverse… As will become understood, the number 33 is a signature of 'they' in their ongoing conspiracy based agenda that 'they' so desperately want the people of the world to feel the consequences of, but not be privy to. Ahead we'll cover the Gematria of 33 for 'false flag' and 'pirate', where the term 'false flag' originates from; and how once upon a time, the very Masonic Knights Templar, were pirates.

Tom = 7+12+14 = 33 (RO); Flo = 6+12+15 = 33 (O)

On the subject of recordings and propaganda, think about all the recorded propaganda available for mainstream consumption that somehow the sleeping masses don't see through. As I write this book, some classic examples we have are the melting planes of September 11 that defied the laws of physics, with their fiberglass wings piercing steel and concrete, at least according to what was shown on 'TV'. We also have the footage of multiple men in army fatigues running out the back of Sandy Hook Elementary School, and then the shooting being blamed on 112-pound Adam Lanza hours later. Days after the incident, the media said this was because they were accidentally showing footage of an active shooter drill at a different elementary school, in close proximity to Sandy Hook, while the Sandy Hook shooting was taking place. Somehow, someway, people buy this. *As for Adam Lanza's weight of 112-pounds, we'll get to why 'they' reported this, a seemingly meaningless detail, until you check the Gematria of 'Sandy Hook'.* Even better, we have the Boston Marathon Bombing smoke-bomb and firework explosions that didn't even disturb the silverware, glasses or plates on the tables they detonated by. Plus, on top of that, there is video evidence of people purposefully manufacturing the fake terror scene, including pouring fake blood on the ground, lead by a man in a cowboy hat, and yet, somehow, someway, people still aren't catching on to the manufactured deception and extremely obvious lies. Sadly, instead,

they're just falling back on their programmed responses; "conspiracy theory", "coincidence", "tinfoil hat".

For another example of the programming that enforces those stereotypical responses, the fast food brand Taco Bell, owned by Yum Foods, began a series of ads titled Belluminati at the end of 2017, mocking the existence of powerful secret societies such as the Illuminati, or simply put, 'they'. The image shown to the left is a clip from the original Belluminati ad, which focuses on the dollar. You'll notice the series of letters and numbers on the dollar bill begins TB, for Taco Bell, then continues with 235 and so on. In light of this series of numbers being emphasized on the dollar bill beginning with 235, I want to show you what is interesting about the Gematria of 'Federal Reserve', the Illuminati owned asset, that prints the U.S. currency, and how it compares with the name Taco Bell was promoting for the commercial, 'Belluminati'.

Federal Reserve = 21+22+23+22+9+26+15+9+22+8+22+9+5+22 = 235 (RO)

Belluminati = 3+10+24+24+42+26+18+28+2+40+18 = 235 (Franc Baconis)

Recall, each leg of the Masonic compasses is kicked out at 23.5-degrees (235), forming a 47-degree angle. This factors into 'Taco Bell', summing to 47 in Reverse Reduction Gematria. Making matters even more interesting is the Gematria of 'Belluminati' in KFW Kabbalah, and the Ordinal Gematria of Bavarian Illuminati, the enlightenment organization established May 1, 1776, just before the American Revolution.

Bavarian   Illuminati   = 2+1+22+1+18+9+1+14+9+12+12+21+13+9+14+1+20+9 = 188 (O)

Belluminati = 20+17+18+18+25+5+23+22+9+8+23 = 188 (KFW Kabbalah)

In light of money being the focus of the commercial, and how many  items you can buy with just $1 at Taco Bell, consider the denominations of U.S. currency; the $1, the $2, the $5, the $10, the $20, the $50, and the $100. If you add each value together, it totals 188, and it is the symbolism of the Bavarian Illuminati on the $1-bill, that is printed by the Federal Reserve. Case and point, the 13-layers of bricks on the dollar are symbolic of the 13-families that established the organization, and the knowledge of the sun, our nearest star, in relation to the 12-constellations.

Speaking of the pyramid with 13-layers of bricks, it reminds why Taco Bell was chosen for such a series of ads. It relates to the company's founding on March 21, 1962, a date with numerology of 86 (3/21/62 = 3+21+62 = 86), the passing of their founder at age 86, who was 'Glen William Bell', a name summing to 86 in Reverse Reduction, and who passed on a date with numerology of 47 (January 16, 2010), as well as their logo, which relates directly to the number 86. If you're not aware, Taco Bell has a pyramid for a logo, and the words 'pyramid', 'triangle', and 'symbol' each equates to 86 in Ordinal Gematria. As for the pyramid on the dollar bill, the eye at the top is known as the 'Eye of Providence', having Reduction Gematria of 86. And as for the 'eye' itself, you learned earlier the word sums to 35 in Ordinal, which corresponds with 'Illuminati' in Septenary, also equating to 35. Consider, the Illuminati attempts to rule the mind's eye of the masses with symbolism. And if you want to go deeper, recall that 35, symbolizing 'eye', is a fascinating number, because 5 is the 3rd prime, and both 3 and 5 are prime numbers as individual digits.

The Illuminati = 20+8+5+9+12+12+21+13+9+14+1+20+9 = 153 (O)

Prime Numbers = 16+18+9+13+5+14+21+13+2+5+18+19 = 153 (O)

Regarding the Illuminati and the 'eye', the symbol shown to the left is often associated with the Bavarian Illuminati. Notice the Gematria of the motto, 'Eye see everything'. In Reverse Ordinal Gematria, that phrase sums to 235, just the same as 'Federal Reserve'. And of course, it is money that is controlling the mind's eye for nearly all of humanity. I often say, *if only we could get people to care about the truth, in the same way they care about dollar dollar bills y'all...*

Eye	See	Everything	=

22+2+22+8+22+22+22+5+22+9+2+7+19+18+13+20 = 235

Speaking of the mind's eye of the masses being controlled, and them not seeing the obvious because of it, in the year 2017, as I write this, on a weekly basis, as the quickening is taking place, we are bombarded with details of "terrorist attacks", accompanied with "witness accounts" of the "terror", by people who are laughing and grinning at the same time, when they are supposed to be providing details of a terrible tragedy. You would think more people would catch on, as routine as these scenarios in the media have become. For example, who can forget Robbie Parker, the first Sandy Hook parent, who was joking and laughing with someone just off camera, before being alerted he was on live television, which prompted him to take a deep breath, and then act as if he was all choked up at the loss of his child?

Parker = 7+1+9+2+5+9 = 33 (R)

Robbie = 9+6+2+2+9+5 = 33 (R)

*Robert = 9+6+2+5+9+2 = 33 (R)

Newtown = 5+5+5+2+6+5+5 = 33 (R) (Location of Sandy Hook 'false flag')

Moments into the theatrical performance, he asked the general public to donate money through his 'Facebook' page, an entity controlled by 'they'. If you have never noticed, Mark Zuckerberg, the Zionist and front man for the CIA controlled social media platform, has the same birthday as Israel, May 14, which we will cover later (Zuck was born in '84, Israel was born in '48). If you are willing, please look up the 2010 D8

Conference interview where Mark Zuckerberg revealed that on the inside of his 'Facebook' hoodies, there are secretly hidden Star of David logos, as shown to the left. Things such as this should break even the most sincere of "coincidence theorists". It is blatant. As for Robbie "The Conman" Parker, can you imagine losing your daughter, telling jokes, laughing, and then suddenly after finding out the cameras were on you, acting as if you're sad, before asking for strangers to send you money?

Notice, that in all of these "terrorist" attacks, and "mass shootings", there is a public fundraiser that comes along with it now, and usually as part of the campaign for raising money, it is the city name, with the word 'strong'; i.e. 'Boston Strong'. This is not by accident; observe how 'strong' has Gematria of 93, corresponding with 'propaganda'.

Strong = 19+20+18+15+14+7 = 93 (O)

Usually in these made for TV propaganda scenarios, there is a paid for media propagandist, who is truly an employee of the CIA, coaching the crisis actor along, such as Anderson Cooper, who shamed all the people speaking truth about the obvious lies of Sandy Hook. Cooper and other perpetrators of fear in the media will often use buzzwords to help these smiling actors and actresses play along to the false tragedy by saying, "Can you tell us about the fear you were feeling?" They love that word, fear. Fear sells, and fear controls. Of course, this is an agenda about control. For a little more Gematria practice, take a moment to decode both of his names, and you'll find 'Anderson' sums to 36 in Reduction, same as 'Cooper'. Recall, 666 is the 36th triangular number, and to go with it, 'Anderson Cooper' in Reverse Ordinal, sums to 216, the product of 6x6x6. Making matters even more interesting, his recorded birthday is June 3, or 3/6. This man, along with every other face you see in the propaganda based news media, is an agent of 'The Beast', same with the rest of the gang of 'they'. And if you're not aware, crisis actors are a big and growing industry, that goons like Cooper speak to each and everyday on the 100% propaganda based airwaves, again funded with our tax dollars, by the CIA, which needs to be put out of commission, as the 33rd President, Harry S. Truman, requested in a Washington Post op -ed, dated December 22, 1963. Of course it was Truman who signed the CIA, NSA, and all the other branches of government into existence, that now work to deceive us and spy on us on the daily. His op-ed, a month after the killing of JFK, was no doubt written because of what transpired November 22, in the "thirty-three" ritual that it was. Please read it, he clearly stated that the CIA needed to be reduced to an intelligence-gathering platform, with NO OTHER 'POWER'. Of course, that never happened, and since then, its biceps have only grown.

On the subject of crisis actors, paid for with CIA dollars, which means your dollars, a name to look up is recent history is 'Joshua Bitsko', the supposed Las Vegas police officer, who began laughing on 60 Minutes, the CBS news program, while describing the room of the shooter in the October 1, 2017 Las Vegas massacre, where he said he was "literally tripping over guns" because there were so many in the room. Someone tell me, what's so funny about destroying a crime scene, or anything else for that matter? Another name to look up is Dr. H. Wayne Carver, the medical examiner who laughed multiple times in a 15-minute press conference about the supposedly 26-deceased at Sandy Hook Elementary in Newtown, Connecticut. The fact that the CIA and media are willing to put out these interviews goes to show, they know just how asleep the zombie-like masses are, who seemingly have lost the ability to reason, or apply logic to what is coming through the screens, from TVs to smartphones. How could a man laugh and smile while talking about dead children? HOW!? I'm being rhetorical. To answer the question, I'll quote the 'orange' oompa loompa, Donald Trump, who said on October 13, 2017, while pledging money to Israel, and at the same time disrespecting the people of 'Puerto Rico', who he said were looking for handouts, only after they had just been slaughtered with a manmade storm, "the United States is a nation of believers!" What that means is we're not a nation of thinkers, which is a deadly problem, literally.

Dr. H. Wayne Carver = 4+9+8+5+1+7+5+5+3+1+9+22+5+9 = 93 (R, V22)

As for 'Joshua Bitsko', his name has multiple connections to Freemasonry and the reported events of October 1, 2017 in Las Vegas, Nevada, which I'll begin to introduce. For one of many, in the Reduction method, his name sums to 42, just the same as 'Freemason'. As a reminder, the divisors of the number 42 equate to 96, and 'Freemason' equates to 42 in Reduction, as well as 96 in Ordinal. Instead of decoding his name further, I will dissect the words 'policeman', 'cop', and as a reminder, 'authority', because routinely these minions of the 'New World Order' (*Hint: Joshua Bitsko = New World Order = False Flag),* are appearing on television, and lying about hoaxes and false flags that are meant to build the agenda of the tyrants at the top, the ongoing police state, the 'Big Brother' mission. As we decode, keep in mind they said the 'Nevada' shooter owned 47-firearms, a familiar number, and one reported by the feds after the ATF first reported he owned '42' guns, the latter count matching the Ordinal Gematria of 'gun', where again, Joshua Bitsko was having trouble not tripping on the guns in the shooter's room. Please know that across the world, police have always been the agents of 'they', which is why police exist. If you doubt what I am saying, pay attention the next time there is a protest against corporate tyranny; you'll notice the police line up to defend the tyrants. It is clockwork and it never fails. For the person who knows their history, they know police were first created to protect rich merchants in 'London', and in every society where police have been formed, crime rates have increased, and not coincidentally. The biggest killers and drug dealers throughout the world are police, and they have been since the time of their existence. The police are your enemy, and to not know this, is to be completely ignorant. Seriously, what do 'they' do besides show up to crime scenes well after the fact, offer no assistance to the victims, and needlessly write tickets and shutdown lanes during rush hour causing extra traffic? As we decode the relevant terms, keep in mind the videogame and movie character, 'Agent 47', from the series *Hitman*.

Agent = 1+7+5+14+20 = 47 (O); Authority = 1+3+2+8+6+9+9+2+7 = 47 (R)

Policeman = 2+3+6+9+6+4+5+8+4 = 47 (RR); Cop = 24+12+11 = 47 (RO)

Government = 2+3+5+4+9+4+5+4+4+7 = 47 (RR)

*Firearm = 3+9+9+4+8+9+5 = 47 (RR); *Nevada = 14+5+22+1+4+1 = 47 (O)

Policeman = 11+3+6+9+6+22+5+8+4 = 74 (RR, P11, E22)

London = 12+15+14+4+15+14 = 74 (O)

Joshua = 10+15+19+8+21+1 = 74 (O) (As in "Joshua Bitsko")

Now is a good time to point out the modern era of Freemasonry began June 24, 1717, with the 'Premier' Grand Lodge of 'London', 'England', on a date with 47 numerology.

Premier = 2+9+4+5+9+4+9 = 42 (RR); Premier = 7+9+5+4+9+5+9 = 48 (R)

Freemason = 6+9+5+5+4+1+1+6+5 = 42 (R); Freemason = 3+9+4+4+5+8+8+3+4 = 48 (RR)

6/24/17 = 6+24+17 = <u>47</u>; *Mason = 17 (R)*

To take it a step further, let us connect 'police' and 'conspiracy'.

Police = 60+50+20+9+3+5 = 147 (Jewish Gematria)

Freemason = 21+9+22+22+14+26+8+12+13 = 147 (RO)

Conspiracy = 24+12+13+8+11+18+9+26+24+2 = 147 (RO)

Masonic = 25+2+38+30+28+18+6 = 147 (Franc Baconis)

162

*Mother's Basement = 5+3+7+10+22+9+8+7+8+8+22+5+22+4+7
= 147 (RR, H10, E22)

Recall, when Kabbalah is practiced within Freemasonry, it is called 'Qabalah'. These police agents are used in every Qabalah based false flag / hoax ritual, without exception. They are sworn minions of The Synagogue of Satan and are used as such, because ultimately, at the top of Freemasonry, the puppeteers of the fraternity are the same false Jews spoken of in the *Bible*. Let us now examine the Gematria of 'Qabalah' and how it connects to 'Gematria' when the Franc Baconis cipher is used. Before decoding, let us examine this quote from Manly P. Hall on the language of Gematria, in relation to Qabalah. His words, from *The Secret Teachings of All Ages,* are as follows. "The three Qabbalistical processes termed Gematria, Notarikon and Temurah makes possible the discovery of many of the profoundest truths of ancient Jewish super-physics." In case you're wondering what Notarikon and Temurah are, they are specific to Hebrew and have to do with rearranging the letters of given words.

Qabalah = 10+26+25+26+15+26+19 = 147 (RO)

Gematria = 13+10+26+2+40+36+18+2 = 147 (Franc Baconis)

As I mentioned earlier, Manly P. Hall earned his top honors in the Scottish Rite of Freemasonry 47-years after writing *The Secret Teachings of All Ages*. In that book he exposes the reader to Ordinal and Reduction Gematria, advising the reader to experiment with Reduction. What he left out were the Reverse methods, plus everything else I have taught you. Let's now decode the title of his book, with Reverse Reduction.

The Secret Teachings of All Ages =
7+1+4+8+4+6+9+4+7+7+4+8+6+1+9+4+2+8+3+3+8+6+6+8+2+4+8
= 147 (RR)

Let us also decode the name 'Manly P. Hall', recognizing how it connects to the Reduction Gematria of 'Freemason', 42. To give credit where it is due, he did teach his readers how to make these very simple calculations. He also shared the method for revealing what is special about the name 'Hall'. If you experiment with the ciphers you have learned, you will see the multiple ways his name also connects to 'Scottish Rite', including having Gematria of 57, one of our numbers connected to 'conspiracy'.

Manly P. Hall = 4+1+5+3+7+7+8+1+3+3 = 42 (R); Hall = 8+1+12+12 = 33 (O)

For good measure, you should know the name 'Qabalah' pairs nicely with 'Freemason' in more ways than one. Keep in mind 'Freemason' sums to 42 in Reduction, 48 in Reverse Reduction, similar to 'Premier', and 'Masonry' sums to 39 in Reverse Reduction as well, not unlike the number of books in the Old Testament, where 39 is also a special number to the Tree of Life, as we learned in Chapter 8.

Qabalah = 17+1+2+1+12+1+8 = 42 (O)

Qabalah = 19+1+20+1+2+1+4 = 48 (ALW Kabbalah)

Qabalah = 1+8+7+8+6+8+10 = 48 (RR, H10)

Qabalah = 1+8+7+8+6+8+1 = 39 (RR)

Qabalah = 4+1+2+1+2+1+6 = 17 (Septenary)

On the subject of Freemasonry and police, all throughout the United States of America, there is a very familiar pattern with police stations being built in close proximity to the town's local Scottish Rite Freemason Lodge, from small towns to large cities. Often times the buildings are right next door, or just across the street from each other. Hardly ever are they more than a few blocks away from one another. This is no 'coincidence'; instead it is because they are essentially one and the same. To be clear, the Scottish Rite of Freemasonry controls all of police, across the world, no exceptions. With all Masonic related things, the Gematria tells the tale.

Fraternal	Order	of	Police	=

3+9+8+7+22+9+4+8+6+3+9+5+22+9+3+3+11+3+6+9+6+22 = 187 (RR, P11, E22)

Ancient Accepted Scottish Rite of Freemasonry =

1+5+3+9+5+5+2+1+3+3+5+7+2+5+4+1+3+6+2+2+9+1+8+9+9+ 2+5+6+6+6+9+5+5+4+1+1+6+5+9+7 = 187 (RR)

How do you think police departments came up with the homicide code, 187, as is used in California and elsewhere? Again, these people want to be like God, or 'Elohim' (מיקולא), summing to 187 in Hebrew, and being the name used commonly in the 187-chapter *Torah*. *Please know this Hebrew spelling of Elohim is an alternate method used by Kabbalists to generate a value of 187, the traditional spelling sums to 47.*

מיקולא = 1+30+6+100+10+40 = 187 (Hebrew Traditional)

The traditional spelling is just below, corresponding with 'authority'. The 'authority' wants to be God, and we the people, have let them become something close, which must be undone, now and not later. For each day that passes, their power builds, and ours diminishes, because this is the steady direction of things. *Hello PATRIOT Act.*

םיהולא = 1+12+6+5+10+13 = 47 (Hebrew Ordinal)

We'll expose the police for what 'they' are many times over as we progress, along with the federal and state governments they serve, but for now, you should also know that in Reduction Gematria, the title of 'police' sums to 33, reminding of the infamous 'LAPD' beating of Rodney King, on March 3, 1991, an event we'll take apart in great detail in the 'race war' chapter. By knowing the code, you'll see just how repetitive the patterns are of the stories in the media, meant to incite racial division, from Rodney King, to OJ Simpson, to Trayvon Martin, to Michael Brown, to Freddie Gray, and so much more.

Police = 7+6+3+9+3+5 = 33 (R); Masonry = 4+1+1+6+5+9+7 = 33 (R)

LAPD = 12+1+16+4 = 33 (O)

For the record, the first 'police' force in 'England', which gives roots to police as we now know them, was known as the 'Marine Police Force', which ties right back into the numbers we have covered, including 33, 47 and 147.

England = 4+4+2+6+8+4+5 = 33 (RR)

Marine = 4+1+9+9+5+5 = 33 (R)

Police = 7+6+3+9+3+5 = 33 (R)

Force = 6+15+18+3+5 = 47 (O)

Marine Police Force = 5+8+9+9+4+4+2+3+6+9+6+4+3+3+9+6+4 = 94 (RR)

Ninety-Four = 14+9+14+5+20+25 + 6+15+21+18 = 147 (O)

Don't forget Revelation 9:4 is the 147th verse of the *Bible*, or that Jacob, who is also known as Israel, dies at age 147, in *Genesis 47*. In the Chapter on World Wars, we'll learn more about the recognition of Israel, in '47, with a 33-member vote in favor, on the 333rd day of the year. And in the chapter on NASA, we'll learn just how important the relationship between 94 and 147 truly is. Also pertinent, recall that when you write out 'forty-seventh', it equates to 147 in Gematria. These are significant numbers to the code, as you're learning, and police are pertinent minions to the Freemasonic, New World Order agenda, as stated, and stated again, for thoroughness.

Now as for the word 'they', the Gematria behind it, in our most basic Ordinal method, reveals the numbers 58, which you became familiar with at the conclusion of Chapter 2.

They = 20+8+5+25 = 58 (O)

Recall how this number connects to 'Freemasonry', as well as 'Rosicrucian' Order, where the roots of modern Freemasonry rest. In a moment we'll discuss the death of King James at age 58, the Rosicrucian and Freemason, whose right hand man, Francis Bacon, has much to do with the establishment of the 'United States' of America. As we decode, recall that 'Rose Cross' is the meaning of the name 'Rosicrucian', and it is a symbol of secrecy.

Freemasonry = 6+9+5+5+4+1+1+6+5+9+7 = 58 (R)

Rosicrucian = 9+6+1+9+3+9+3+3+9+1+5 = 58 (R)

Rose Cross = 9+3+8+4+6+9+3+8+8 = 58 (RR)

Fraternal = 3+9+8+7+4+9+4+8+6 = 58 (RR)

Secret Society = 1+5+3+9+5+2+1+6+3+9+5+2+7 = 58 (R)

Solomon's Temple = 1+6+3+6+4+6+5+1+2+5+4+7+3+5 = 58 (R)

Herod's Temple = 1+4+9+3+5+8+7+4+5+2+6+4 = 58 (RR)

Jerusalem = 8+4+9+6+8+8+6+4+5 = 58 (RR)

Craftsman = 6+9+8+3+7+8+5+8+4 = 58 (RR)

United States = 3+5+9+2+5+4+10+2+1+2+5+10 = 58 (R, S10)

Washington = 5+1+10+8+9+5+7+2+6+5 = 58 (R, S10)

We The People = 5+5+2+8+5+7+5+6+7+3+5 = 58 (R)

In God We Trust = 9+5+7+6+4+5+5+2+9+3+1+2 = 58 (R)

Annuit Coeptis = 1+5+5+3+9+2+3+6+5+7+2+9+1 = 58 (R)

Don't Tread On Me = 4+6+5+2+2+9+5+1+4+6+5+4+5 = 58 (R)

*Susan G. Komen = 10+3+10+1+5 + 7 + 2+6+4+5+5 = 58 (R, S10)

Power = 11+12+4+22+9 = 58 (RO)

Press = 11+9+22+8+8 = 58 (RO)

Big Brother = 7+9+2+7+9+3+7+1+4+9 = 58 (O)

Facebook = 6+1+3+5+2+15+15+11 = 58 (O)

For you Freemasons out there, did you complete your three tracing boards for your first three degrees, what are in relation to the 'biblical' story of *Jacob's Ladder* from *Genesis?* They probably forgot to tell you about Gematria when you signed up, am I right?

Tracing Board = 2+9+1+3+9+5+7+2+6+1+9+4 = 58 (R)

Biblical = 7+9+7+6+9+6+8+6 = 58 (RR); *Pagans = 16+1+7+1+14+19 = 58 (O)

And regarding "conspiracy theory", this is where our complimentary ciphers kick in.

Conspiracy Theory = 3+2+1+6+3+5+5+1+3+2+7+6+5+2+5+2 = 58 (Septenary)

Conspiracy Theory = 3+7+5+3+8+1+2+1+3+1+4+5+5+7+2+1 = 58 (Chaldean)

Again, we're not talking conspiracy theory here, we're talking strictly conspiracy fact, and these Freemasons at the head of the conspiracy are absolutely up *Doo-doo Creek without a paddle* because of the repetitiveness of their rituals causing harm to the people of the world, and because since 2013, the knowledge of their wrongdoing, by the numbers, has been exposed by yours truly, at an ever increasing rate, that is about to reach a critical mass, bringing their reign to a long overdue end. As stated, this reign goes back to before the establishment of the United States of America, which is where we'll now revisit. If you are not familiar with Francis Bacon (we learned a bit about him in Chapter 3, in relation to Shakespeare), the right hand man of King James, who was also a Rosicrucian and Freemason, and who is credited for being the

"The Guiding Spirit in the Colonization Scheme", a motto remembered on collector stamps from the year 1610, that were used in England.

It is said Francis Bacon, being a man of wisdom and influence, persuaded Queen Elizabeth I, who became Queen in 1558, emphasis on '58, to fund the voyages that began the early colonizing of what became the 'United States' of America, a mission completed 166-years after the 1610 stamps were created. Not by chance, 'secret society' in Ordinal Gematria sums to 166, and so does 'The Guiding Spirit in the Colonization Scheme' when the Septenary cipher is applied. Also, as we learned, there is nothing arbitrary about the date July 4, 1776, in light of the 'Masonic' nation that is 'America', established by the secret brotherhood. Let us also decode the name of the plan for the early formation of the nation, the 'Colonization Scheme', a title summing to 58 in the Septenary cipher, *go figure.*

Colonization   Scheme   =
3+2+2+2+1+5+1+1+7+5+2+1+6+3+6+5+1+5 = 58 (Septenary)

The Guiding Spirit in the Colonization Scheme = 166 (Septenary)

Secret Society = 19+5+3+18+5+20+19+15+3+9+5+20+25 = 166 (O)

The   Bavarian   Illuminati   =
7+10+22+7+8+5+8+9+9+8+4+9+6+6+6+5+9+4+8+7+9 = 166 (RR, H10, E22)

As for Francis Bacon, also known as Lord Bacon, I want to examine his date of birth, and his date of death, to reveal something extremely fascinating about his legacy, and the nation that would go on to become 'The United States of America'. Francis Bacon was born January 22, 1561, and died April 9, 1626, unexpectedly from pneumonia, preventing him from finishing his written work, *'New Atlantis'*, a title we learned a bit about in the opening chapter. There are multiple fascinating components here, but we'll begin with the number 99, as Francis Bacon died on the 99th day of the calendar year. As we decode his birth numerology, you'll notice it connects to the numbers 99 as well as 84, numbers both having much to do with the United States of America.

1/22/1561 = 1+22+15+61 = 99; 1/22/61 = 1+22+61 = 84

In Reduction Gematria, 'The United States of America' sums to 99, and if you leave off 'The', the name of the nation totals 84.

The United States of America = 2+8+5+3+5+9+2+5+4+1+2+1+2+5+1+6+6 +1+4+5+9+9+3+1 = 99 (R)

United States of America = 3+5+9+2+5+4+1+2+1+2+5+1+6+6 +1+4+5+9+9+3+1 = 84 (R)

If you use the Franc Baconis cipher, one credited to Francis Bacon, 'America' also equates to 99. *The same is also true of 'Scottish Rite' in LCH Kabbalah.*

America = 1+26+10+36+18+6+2 = 99 (Franc Baconis)

Scottish Rite = 15+2+10+9+9+0+15+3+14+0+9+13 = 99 (LCH Kabbalah)

Think about how the nation began with 13-colonies, and the flag has 13-stripes, and once 13-stars. In Ordinal Gematria, 'thirteen' also sums to 99.

Thirteen = 20+8+9+18+20+5+5+14 = 99 (O); Star = 1+2+1+9 = 13 (R)

Also relevant, in the Franc Baconis cipher, what is found on the collector's stamp, equates to 909, not too far off from '99'.

The Guiding Spirit in the Colonization Scheme = 39+16+10+13+42+18+8+18+28+14+37+32+18+36+18+40+18+28+40+16+10+5+30+24
+30+28+18+52+2+40+18+30+28+37+6+16+10+26+10 = 909 (Franc Baconis)

His April 9 death on the 99th day of the year can be expressed 4/9, something like 49.

The number 49 points directly to America as well.

America = 8+5+4+9+9+6+8 = 49 (RR); *Washington = 49 (R)

When he died April 9, it was 77-days after his birthday, a number connecting to 'United States', 'Secret Society', 'power', and also the number 49. As we decode, don't forget Washington D.C. is on the 77th Meridian West.

United States = 6+4+9+7+4+5+8+7+8+7+4+8 = 77 (RR)

Secret Society = 8+4+6+9+4+7+8+3+6+9+4+7+2 = 77 (RR)

Power = 16+15+23+5+18 = 77 (O)

Seventy-Seven = 1+5+4+5+5+2+7+1+5+4+5+5 = 49 (R)

Power = 11+3+4+22+9 = 49 (RR, P11, E22)

As mentioned, Francis Bacon was known as 'Lord Bacon'. This title has Gematria of 84 in Ordinal, as does 'Colony', as does 'States'. In Reverse Ordinal, Masonry also sums to

Equally as important, the word 'Jesuit' in Ordinal sums to 84, and at the point in history when Bacon died, the Rosicrucian Order and the Jesuits were said to be sworn enemies, at war with each other. While that might have been true then, it is very clear they're in bed together in the modern age, as allies in the New World Order agenda, part of what Manly P. Hall called the Order of the Quest.

Lord Bacon = 12+15+18+4 + 2+1+3+15+14 = 84 (O)

Colony = 3+15+12+15+14+25 = 84 (O); States = 19+20+1+20+5+19 = 84 (O)

Masonry = 14+26+8+12+13+9+2 = 84 (RO) (*M = 84, Reverse Sumerian)

The Jesuit Order = 7+1+4+8+4+8+6+9+7+3+9+5+4+9 = 84 (RO)

Jesuit = 10+5+19+21+9+20 = 84 (O)

The Catholic Church = 2+8+5+3+1+2+8+6+3+9+3+3+8+3+9+3+8 = 84 (R)

Again, Francis Bacon was the 'Guiding Spirit' of the 'Colonization Scheme'.

The Guiding Spirit = 7+6+5+7+6+5+4+5+1+7+6+3+5+5+5+7 = 84 (Septenary)

On the subject of 84, there is a parallel with the number 40, and again, it is the spelling within the *King James Bible* of 'forty' that is the reason we still spell the word as is today. Notice how when 'forty' is written out, it has a Gematria of 84, and further, how 40 also pertains to the 'United States', 'U.S.', 'U.S.A.' as well as 'Old Testament,' what is the majority of the Bible, including the *King James Bible.*

Forty = 6+15+18+20+25 = 84 (O); U.S. = 21+19 = 40 (O); U.S.A. = 6+8+26 = 40 (RO)

United States = 3+5+9+2+5+4+1+2+1+2+5+1 = 40 (R)

Old Testament = 6+3+4+2+5+1+2+1+4+5+5+2 = 40 (R)

* By the book = 2+7+2+8+5+2+6+6+2 = 40 (R); Mathematics = 40 (R)

Using the Septenary cipher, his unfinished written work 'New Atlantis' also sums to 40.

New Atlantis = 1+5+4+1+7+2+1+1+7+5+6 = 40 (Septenary)

Atlantis = 1+2+3+1+5+2+9+10 = 33 (R, S10); Americas = 1+4+5+9+9+3+1+1 = 33 (R)

Speaking of Francis Bacon's written work, 'New Atlantis', there is something very fascinating about the title that syncs with the number 99 just as well. As we decode, consider he died while writing the text. In Satanic Gematria, New Atlantis sums to 523, the 99th prime number.

New Atlantis = 49+40+58+36+55+47+36+49+55+44+54 = 523 (Satanic Gematria)

I should mention the oldest known Freemason meeting traces back to July 31, 1599, emphasis on '99, at the 'Lodge of Edinburgh'. In Ordinal Gematria, the name of the lodge sums to 152, matching the date numerology of the meeting. In addition, 'Edinburgh' sums to 47 in Reverse Reduction, the number we know well.

*7/31/1599 = 7+31+15+99 = 152

As for his book, it was about a utopian 'empire'. Fittingly, in Reduction, 'New Atlantis' and 'empire' have Gematria of 39, matching the numbers of books in the Old Testament, which he had a hand in writing for King James. His alias, 'Lord Bacon' also equates to the same number in the same method.

New Atlantis = 5+5+5+1+2+3+1+5+2+9+1 = 39 (R); Empire = 5+4+7+9+9+5 = 39 (R)

Lord Bacon = 3+6+9+4 + 2+1+3+6+5 = 39 (R)

His date of death also had numerology of 39, leaving *New Atlantis* unfinished (*4+9+26 = 39*). Not too far off from 39, is the number 139, which is what the name 'Francis' equates to using the Franc Baconis cipher.

Francis = 11+36+2+28+6+18+38 = 139 (Franc Baconis)

This number is important to 'Freemasonry', 'America' and more. If you've ever seen the TV show 'West World', it factors right in, because it is about a land where people live, who unknown to them, the purpose of their existence is not their own. If you read what is within the *Talmud,* where it says the goyim is to slave for the Jewish master, the pieces really begin to fall into place.

Freemasonry = 6+18+5+5+13+1+19+15+14+18+25 = 139 (O)

America = 26+14+22+9+18+24+26 = 139 (RO)

West World = 23+5+19+20+23+15+18+12+4 = 139 (O)

Jewish State = 10+5+23+9+19+8+19+20+1+20+5 = 139 (O)

Jerusalem = 17+22+9+6+8+26+15+22+14 = 139 (O)

The Bavarian Illuminati = 7+1+4+7+8+5+8+9+9+8+4+9+6+6+6+5+9+4+8+7+9 = 139 (RR)

Remember, the Kabbalah code, which all of this is based in, traces back to Jerusalem. And better than that, in *New Atlantis* a Jew named 'Joabin', who Francis Bacon is sure to mention, is circumcised, assists the protagonist. *Joabin = 8+3+8+7+9+4 = 39 (RR)*

Better than that, the name Joabin also encodes '666'. Recall in Chapter 3, we learned about the Psalm 46 tribute in the *King James Bible*, where the 46th word is Shake, and the 46th word from the end is Spear, and how Psalm 46 leaves 666 remaining chapters in the *KJV* of 1611, the year of its first publishing, hinting that Shakespeare was indeed Bacon.

Joabin = 102+72+156+150+108+78 = 666 (Reverse Sumerian)

In Jewish history books, it is well taught that the United States of America is a Jewish nation, from its inception. As Jewish historians will write, if it was not for Jewish bankers, the 'Revolutionary War' would have never been able to be fought, because it was Jewish bankers who paid for America to engage the battle. If you have *Netflix,* there is a film you can stream called *Four Blood Moons* that delves into this subject.

Revolutionary War = 9+5+4+6+3+3+2+9+6+5+1+9+7+5+1+9 = 84 (R)

Revolutionary War = 5+5+5+2+2+6+7+5+2+1+1+5+2+4+1+5 = 58 (Septenary)

Of course, from that point in history, up to the present, all wars, across all of the world, have been funded by Jewish bankers, who love the interest war lending generates for them. Have you ever noticed how 'new' rhymes with 'Jew'? Again, this is the New World Order, which is really a quite old world order at this point. In the Talmud, charging interest is permitted, something that is frowned on in the other religions of the world. Recall, Jesus didn't have nice things to say about the 'moneychangers', a title having Ordinal Gematria of 147, not unlike 'one dollar', which sums to 147 in Reverse Ordinal, as well as 96 in Ordinal.

For a few last points about 'Francis', before we move on to King James whom he served, I want you to see how the name 'Francis' connects to 'U.S.A.'. As you learned in Chapter 3, the name has Gematria of 119, connecting to the Reverse Reduction Gematria of 'William Shakespeare'. When you use the Francis Bacon method of Gematria, U.S.A. also sums to 119, connecting to 'Orthodox', 'Star of David', and 'All Seeing Eye'.

Francis = 21+9+26+13+24+18+8 = 119 (RO); U.S.A. = 47+45+27 = 119 (Francis Bacon)

The name 'Francis' also reminds of the date of establishment for the United States of America, as well as the degrees on the compasses of the Freemason logo.

Francis = 3+9+8+4+6+9+8 = 47 (RR)

And in Jewish Gematria his name sums to 229, what is the 50th prime, syncing well with 'America' and its 50-states.

Francis = 6+80+1+40+3+9+90 = 229 (Jewish Gematria); America = 50 (O)

His last name, 'Bacon', provides the perfect transition to 'King James', the King who became a Freemason April 15, 1601, and a span of 66-days from turning age 35. That came in history years after he acquired the throne at just 13-months of age, which should clue you in to the fact that the Kings of then, were no different than the puppet Presidents and leaders of the New World Order today. As for James becoming a Freemason when he did, in Jewish Gematria, 'King' sums to 66, and in Ordinal, 'empire' equates to 66 just the same, and James would go on to build an empire. As for April 15, a very specific date, on the Gregorian calendar, it is the 105 th day of the year, which is a number corresponding with the Ordinal Gematria of 'Masonry' and 'Francis Bacon', which both equate to 105, as does 'Zionism', a newer term, but an age old movement, which is the movement of Jewish supremacy. One wonders how much influence Francis Bacon had on King James making this decision, at this specific age and date he did? And a better question than that, in light of his Jewish protagonist in *New Atlantis,* who did Bacon truly serve? I imagine it was the same people the U.S. Presidents serve today, the Kings of Israel, or, The Synagogue of Satan.

Bacon = 2+1+3+15+14 = 35 (O); King James = 2+9+5+7+1+1+4+5+1 = 35 (R)

Masonry = 48+36+54+50+49+53+60 = 350 (Satanic)

Francis Bacon = 6+18+1+14+3+9+19 + 2+1+3+15+14 = 105 (O)

Masonry = 13+1+19+15+14+18+25 = 105 (O)

For the record, it is recorded in what is known as 'The Mutual Agreement' of December 24, 1658, emphasis on '58, at Lodge No. 3 in Perth, Scotland, that April 15, 1601 was the date King James became a Freemason. In Reduction Gematria, the title of the agreement equates to 74, representing 'Masonic'.

The Mutual Agreement = 2+8+5+4+3+2+3+1+3+1+7+9+5+5+4+5+5+2 = 74 (R)

The Bavarian Illuminati = 7+6+5+2+1+5+1+5+5+1+1+5+2+2+6+1+5+1+1+7+5 = 74 (Septenary)

For our final point on Bacon, notice how in Jewish Gematria, Bacon sums to 96, a number we learned earlier represents 'Freemason' in Ordinal. As a reminder, the word 'Free' in Jewish Gematria also sums to 96. It isn't hard to see who is really 'free', in the United States of America, or should I say 'West World'? For anyone reading who would contend they're free in the United States, I would ask you how that is? Did you get to choose to go to school, where you learned about the Jew, Christopher Columbus, who "discovered" a land where people already lived, before beginning the genocide? Did you get to choose what manmade vaccines were injected into your body, as a requirement to attend said schools? Tell me what day was it where you didn't need a dollar to get by? If you start thinking, you'll realize this is a slave state. If your response is, "Well, it could be worse", I would ask you to consider what kind of response that is? Remember, in the *Talmud,* it states the goyim are a lesser race, and they are happy being slaves to the Jew.

Bacon = 2+1+3+50+40 = 96 (Jewish Gematria); Free = 6+80+5+5 = 96 (Jewish)

The Guiding Spirit = 2+8+5+7+3+9+4+9+5+7+1+7+9+9+9+2 = 96 (R)

As for King James, he was the first King to unite the three kingdoms of Ireland, Scotland, and England, doing so after the death of Queen Elizabeth in 1603, and beginning the legacy of what is now known as the United Kingdom, which later expanded into the United States, two entities that have never truly separated, despite the lives lost in the Revolutionary War. For 22-years, James was the King over these 3-specific kingdoms. Notice, 22-years, 3-kingdoms. We've learned a good deal about 223, as well as its reflection 322. In the language of Satanic Gematria, 'James' also equates to 223.

James = 45+36+48+40+54 = 223 (Satanic Gematria)

Of course James did not rule any longer because of his premature death, which came 3-days after the 22-year anniversary of his unprecedented reign over the 3-kingdoms, beginning March 24, 1603 with Elizabeth I's passing. In light of him dying 23-years after becoming a Freemason, and 22-years after ruling over 3-kingdoms, let us decode the word 'king' with Reduction and Reverse Reduction Gematria.

King = 2+9+5+7 = 23 (R); King = 7+9+4+2 = 22 (RR)

King James died March 27, 1625, a fitting date for a 'royal' death. Let us examine.

3/27/1625 = 3+27+16+25 = 71; Royal = 18+15+25+1+12 = 71 (O)

3/27/1625 = 3+2+7+1+6+2+5 = 26; Royal = 9+6+7+1+3 = 26 (R)

In more recent times, on October 21, 2017, the day leaving 71-days left in the year, it was a historic moment when the past 5 still living U.S. Presidents were all gathered in a room together, who will all be offed in due time by the numbers, just as Ronald Reagan was, and the rest of them, which we'll get to. Those 5 men were Barack Obama, George W. Bush, Bill Clinton, George H.W. Bush, and Jimmy Carter. As our papers often tell us, the U.S. Presidents are all connected to royal blood, because as I have mentioned, we do not live in a democracy, we live in a Masonic dictatorship; and Masonry is the order of the elites. On that same date the Presidents gathered, there were headlines about Donald Trump planning to release classified documents on the assassination of JFK. Remember, JFK was the 35th President, the only 'Catholic'. In Reduction, Catholic sums to 35, and in Ordinal, Catholic equates to 71. I make this point to remind you how the same rituals persist, from the time of King James, to the time of King Chump, I mean Trump.

The date of King James's passing, is also the 86th day of the year on the Gregorian calendar. I'm sure you have heard the term 86'd before, tracing back to Walter Winchell's 1933 newspaper column, where he taught it was an alternative way to say 'nix', or get rid of. In all reality, I think the term probably traces back much further than that, despite what the history books say. In Gematria, 'blood sacrifice' sums to 86 in Reverse Reduction, and at the same time, so do the words 'symbol', 'triangle' and 'pyramid' when Ordinal Gematria is used, as we mentioned when discussing the death of the Taco Bell founder; and of course, King James is quite symbolic, having his own *Bible* and all.

178

Regarding his death by the numbers, it is important to point out he died in the year '25, where in Reverse Reduction, 'death' equates to 25.

Recognizing that King James was murdered by the code, as so many in history have been, know this is the code of 'they', and a code that persists to this very day, and will continue to persist, until The Synagogue of Satan is laid to rest, what are the controlling forces of Freemasonry, which in high places, is the New World Order. Let us now examine how the title 'King James' equates to 'ritual sacrifice', then we will examine a recent example of a celebrity being taken by the same numbers.

King James = 16+18+13+20+17+26+14+22+8 = 154 (RO)

*Scottish Rite of Freemasonry = 10+3+6+2+2+9+10+8+9+9+2+5+6+6+6+9+5+5+4+1+10+6+5+9+7 = 154 (R, S10)

Ritual Sacrifice = 18+9+20+21+1+12 + 19+1+3+18+9+6+9+3+5 = 154 (O)

More recently, on June 8, or 8/6, James W. Hardy III (and yes W. is his middle name), a former professional NFL football player, also baring the name James, was found dead in the Indiana River. As I covered then, he was sacrificed for the current living King James, LeBron James, during the time of the 2016-17 NBA Finals, who a year earlier had won his first NBA Championship for Cleveland, Ohio, on the real King James's birthday. Notice how 'James W. Hardy III' equates to 154 as well.

James W. Hardy III = 10+1+13+5+19 + 23 + 8+1+18+4+25 + 9+9+9 = 154 (O)

He died a span of 166-days from his birthday, that number connecting to 'secret society', and if you write 'James Hardy' alone, how he was known in the NFL, it sums to 166 in Reverse Ordinal. As for where he died, in 'Indiana', it has Ordinal Gematria of 52, connecting to 'death', and 'Kabbalah'. It is also a number that connects to the *King James Bible,* where historians concur it was released on the date May 2, 1611, a day that can be written 5/2, similar to 52.

Regarding the *KJV 1611,* as a reminder, that was the year the King turned 45-years old. As we learned earlier, *'Holy Bible'* equates to 45 in Reduction Gematria, as well as Reverse Reduction, matching the Reduction Gematria of 'Geometry' and 'Shakespeare', among other things. Another important reminder is that 'Good Book' sums to 223 in Jewish Gematria, similar to 'James' summing to 223 in Satanic Gematria. As for the May 2 release date, the number 52, in addition to connecting to 'Kabbalah', connects to 'authority' and 'government', and here we're talking about a *Bible* in the name of a King. Even more interesting, May 2, 1611, was 48-days before his 45th birthday, June 19, 1611, having been born June 19, 1566. In Ordinal Gematria, 'James' sums to 48, and again, the number 223 is the 48th prime. As a reminder, Freemason in English and Hebrew (וֹזְסָמ) equates to 48 as well. As for the reflection of 48, which is 84, 'Good Book' has Ordinal Gematria of 84, the number very relevant to Francis Bacon, the credited main author.

James = 10+1+13+5+19 = 48 (O); Freemason = 3+9+4+4+5+8+8+3+4 = 48 (RR)

וֹזְסָמ = 13+15+6+14 = 48 (Hebrew Ordinal)

Another fascinating point about the date May 2 is that on the Gregorian calendar, it is the 122nd day of the year, which corresponds with the word 'Freemason' in Francis Bacon Gematria, ever so fitting. The word 'Elohim' in Jewish Gematria also sums to 122, and in Hebrew Gematria, it is the word Elohim, from the *Bible,* from the first verse of *Genesis* that is the most studied. Don't forget that Francis Bacon was born January 22, a date that can be expressed as 1/22, not unlike 122.

Freemason = 32+18+5+5+13+1+19+15+14 = 122 (Francis Bacon)

Elohim = 5+20+50+8+9+30 = 122 (Jewish Gematria)

With regards to 122, it should also be noted that the establishment date of the Bavarian Illuminati, a 'they' organization, was May 1, 1776, in a leap-year, thus May 1 was the 122nd day of the year. This matters because the number 122 is the reflection of 221, and 'The Bavarian Illuminati' sums to 221 in Ordinal Gematria. To show you a recent example of how these two numbers came together, on March 1, a date that can be expressed as 1/3, not unlike 13, and reminding of the 13 families that established the order, the news was dominated with headlines of Donald Trump's Security Advisor's planned departure, who was H.R. McMaster, an absurd name, and at the same time, a new property scandal involving his daughter, 'Ivanka' Trump. Not by coincidence, this news came on McMaster's 221st day of being 55-years-old, and 122-days after Ivanka Trump's 36th birthday. At the same time, let us not forget that Donald Trump became President on the 221st day of his age, January 20, 2017. Again, as mentioned, every single day, news is contrived by the code, and it often pays tribute to those who are in control of the contriving, 'they'. Of course, "elections" are fixed in the same manner.

Coming back to May 2, or 5/2, not unlike 52, what is the 122nd day of the year in non-leap-years, 'NWO', the common abbreviation for New World Order, equates to 52 in Ordinal Gematria, corresponding with the release date of the *Bible* in the King's name. If you have ever read the *Bible,* you well know it is a book that preps the mind for the current world setting in which we live, where the reader is instructed to obey their kings, obey their government, pay their taxes, and be a good slave, among other things. Personally, these are clear signs to me that the book as we know it has been tampered with by the 'authority', who are interested in control over the masses, or from the controllers perspective, control over the 'goyim'. Honestly, do you think God would really give instructions that it is okay to beat slaves, blackening the eye and loosening the teeth, so long as you don't kill them? This is written in the *Bible* and for the people who accept it as the word of God

181

I have pity. Don't get me wrong, the *Bible* is full of wisdom, and does teach the reader how to mostly live right, but it also gives plenty of advice that is cringe worthy, and reveals it was written by man. Beyond the things that God would clearly not write, is the purposeful encoding we have revealed. Speaking of which, let us acknowledge how 'King James' in the Septenary cipher, corresponds with the Gematria of 33 for 'Bible', 'Good Book', 'Sunday' and 'believe'.

King James = 3+5+1+7+4+1+1+5+6 = 33 (Septenary); James = 8+8+5+4+8 = 33 (RR)

Let us now close with Revelation 13:16-18, about receiving the mark, which codes the plan of the New World Order. As we read the verse, understand this plan is being achieved at this very moment due to "gullible goyim" already beginning to accept RFID chips, which are being promoted as a way of safekeeping their children, in case they are ever kidnapped, something the fear based media constantly reminds parents of, who mostly no longer allow their children to play outside, thanks to the work of 'they'. In addition to parents chipping their children, some prisoners are also receiving RFID chips for tracking purposes, and as a deterrent from trying to escape. Now, without further ado, the *Bible* verses, which are absolutely encoded with what we can refer to as the 'King James' code, are as follows.

Revelation 13:16-18 King James Version (KJV)

16 And he causeth all, both small and great, rich and poor, free and bond, to receive a mark in their **right hand**, or in their **foreheads**:

17 And that no man might buy or sell, save he that had the mark, or the name of the beast, or the number of his name.

18 Here is wisdom. Let him that hath understanding count the number of the beast: for it is the number of a man; and his number is Six hundred threescore and six.

| Revelation | Thirteen | Sixteen | = |

9+5+22+5+3+1+2+9+6+5+2+8+9+9+2+5+5+5+10+9+6+2+5+5+5 =
154 (R, S10, V22)

Right Hand = 9+18+20+19+7+19+26+13+23 = 154 (RO)

Forehead = 21+12+9+22+19+22+26+23 = 154 (RO)

King James = 16+18+13+20+17+26+14+22+8 = 154 (RO)

It is also interesting to note that the name 'King James' has Satanic Gematria of 404, like the number of verses in Revelation, which are 404 in count.

King James = 46+44+49+42 + 45+36+48+40+54 = 404 (Satanic)

And for a final point, notice how 'number of the beast' corresponds with 'New World Order', who is 'they'.

| Number | of | the | Beast | = |

14+21+13+2+5+18+15+6+20+8+5+2+5+1+19+20 = 174 (O)

New World Order = 14+5+23+23+15+18+12+4+15+18+4+5+18 = 174 (O)

| Number | of | the | Beast | = |

50+300+40+2+5+90+60+6+200+8+5+2+5+1+100+200   =   1074
(English Extended)

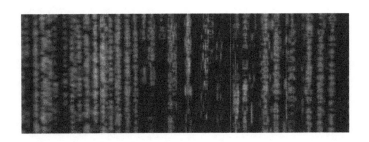

183

Made in the USA
Las Vegas, NV
03 August 2024

93327743R00114